C000127991

BITE SIZED
PEACE

CHANGE HOW YOU EAT.
ACCEPT YOUR BODY.
TRANSFORM YOUR LIFE.

DR ROMI RAN

ISBN: 979-8-9885270-0-8

Disclaimer: This book is intended to provide guidance and information on the relationship between food, eating habits, and the body. It is not a substitute for professional medical or psychological advice, diagnosis, or treatment. The content herein is not intended to replace the guidance of qualified healthcare providers. The author is not responsible for any actions taken by readers based on the content of this book. If you have specific health concerns, it is strongly recommended that you consult with a qualified healthcare professional for personalized guidance.

TABLE OF CONTENTS

PROLOGUE
THE FIRST BITE: HOW IT ALL BEGAN

For over 15 years, I have dedicated my life towards understanding, researching, and working with individuals who experience challenges with their eating, dieting, and body image. Throughout my journey, I've witnessed a diverse range of experiences, such as working with anorexic patients whose bodies were on the verge of failing - to assisting individuals labelled as "morbidly obese," who were coping with profound consequences to their physical, social, and mental health. Moreover, I've encountered patients who didn't neatly fall into a clinical category but were clearly struggling with eating, yo-yo dieting, bingeing, and poor body image–fighting a daily battle with food and their own self-perception.

My entry into this field however, was quite unusual. It stemmed from both a *lack* of exposure to and understanding of eating disorders. Growing up, I would have naively said that I had never personally met anyone suffering from such disorders, and my knowledge was limited to distant sources like celebrities, media, and general discussions. Of course, in retrospect, I realise I did know many people who were wrestling with eating disorders and body dysmorphia, and a larger number who were navigating more subtle, yet significant, struggles with food and body image. What I would come to understand later in life is the staggering extent to which these issues affect a wide variety of people.

My undergraduate studies solidified my fascination with eating and body related difficulties. As we had teachings on the topic, I found myself intrigued by the strong "willpower" of anorexics who didn't eat, as well as the unfamiliar behaviour of individuals making themselves sick after meals. I also found myself immersed in learning about the various factors and behaviours that contribute to obesity, as well as the extreme and obsessive exercise routines pursued in the pursuit of physical transformation. Yet despite my interest, for many years my understanding remained rooted in a sense of separation. I mistakenly believed that individuals with "diagnosed disorders" were a distinct group; distinct from both myself and the rest of those who I perceived as "normal." It was *they* who were the subjects of my investigation, study, and research–the ones *I* sought to aid. And so, with this perspective in hand, my path as a psychologist began to take shape.

The sense of separation I was holding was soon to be shattered, however. I distinctly recall the day when everything shifted–an incident that, on the surface, seemed like a mere exchange, but would later crystallise as a pivotal moment, fundamentally altering my personal understanding and shaping the trajectory of my professional practice.

I had recently moved from the United Kingdom to Boston, Massachusetts. I was walking home one evening with a work colleague, who was also a close friend. She was tall and slender with striking attractiveness accentuated by flowing dark hair that framed her face. Her radiant smile and warm demeanour not only made her stand out in a crowd but also quickly drew people in. We shared many similar interests, personally and professionally, and had a friendship where we could talk for hours about anything. Having only just relocated from across the Atlantic, this close bond was something I deeply cherished. As we were strolling on this warm June evening, an ice cream shop came into view. "Can we stop here for a moment?" my friend asked, as we reached the entrance. We went inside and she placed her order: "I'll have a large, family-sized tub of raspberry and mint swirl ice cream, please."

A few moments later, the counter server handed her the large tub in a white paper bag. As we walked outside, my friend grabbed a bright pink plastic take-away spoon the size of my pinky finger. We stood on the sidewalk and she opened the tub, struggling at first to get the lid off. Once opened, she piled a large scoop onto the tiny spoon. She then took her first mouthful. Her eyes rolled back as she let out a moan of delight. This was followed by an equally full second scoop before she closed the lid and put the tub back into the paper bag.

"That's it?" I asked, intrigued.

"Yes," she responded. **"I just eat what I want, and stop when I've had enough."**

At that precise moment, her seemingly casual response became a profound revelation, forever transforming my perspective on food and eating. I wasn't quite the person who would regularly consume an entire tub of ice-cream in one go (though undoubtedly occurrences of excessive eating did happen), but I also had almost no awareness of *eating what I want* and *stopping when I'd had enough*. In fact, I don't think I would really have even known what enough was–particularly when it came to things like ice cream.

It suddenly occurred to me that my eating habits and food preferences were shaped by ingrained patterns, beliefs, external influences, and some genetic predisposition, rather than a genuine understanding of my own needs. I could see how, as a young woman in my early twenties, I had been conditioned by societal constructs emphasising thinness as an ideal. I had unconsciously accepted body shaming from the public eye and the obsession over what people should or shouldn't eat. Naturally, I felt uncomfortable with certain foods, ice cream being a prime example. Such foods were "naughty treats" and really belonged to special occasions. If I did eat them, I never contemplated if I had actually had enough. Rather, there were rules, expectations, and "all or nothing" thinking. In fact, when I really looked at it, I could see how much of my food and eating choices were simply binary and automatic. I was either trying to "eat well" by choosing food deemed healthy and not over-indulging, or I could opt to "let loose," by guiltily allowing myself to eat, *and often overeat*, foods that I labelled "bad." The former gave me a sense of control and pride, whilst the latter was almost always associated with catastrophizing or feeling guilty by what or how much I had eaten. The interesting thing was that this had all seemed quite normal and in line with what everyone else was experiencing.

All of a sudden, my own relationship to food and eating was being questioned. Was my connection with nourishment and meals truly healthy, caring, and genuine? Or was I simply following a set of rigid rules and conditioned responses? Did I attempt to control what I ate and how I ate, all in a futile attempt to mould my body into a specific shape-one that society and culture deemed acceptable, or even desirable? I started to see that aside from severity, the ideas and behaviours of the ones with diagnoses and disorders were not actually that different from most "normal" people-or from me. In fact, the only real difference was that the ones "*out there*" were (only sometimes) a little more extreme, so they got labelled with a diagnosis. A harsh reality became very clear to me: **Dysfunctional behaviour is completely acceptable, as long as it only occurs an acceptable amount.**

This marked a new start of my personal and professional journey into the intricate world of food, eating, body image, and beyond. What began with the extremities of working with individuals with diagnoses, now shifted to focusing on the more subtle aspects of how *all people* deal with food, eating, and body image. And then even further.

What I have seen consistently throughout my work is that the journey towards healing from disordered eating goes far beyond just changing what someone eats or how they feel about their body. It becomes a gateway to developing a deeper sense of self-awareness, resilience, compassion, and acceptance. Ultimately, it is a path toward shedding unhelpful habits and behaviours rotted in ego-driven thoughts and actions, empowering us to face life's challenges with grace and authenticity.

Over the years, I have used this relationship as a tool for clients who came to me with a range of challenges, mental health concerns, relationship difficulties, and dissatisfaction with life. I have consistently found that exploring clients' relationship with their food and their bodies provided a pathway to profound insights, even when it seemed, at first glance, unrelated to their initial concerns. I have witnessed that the skills and techniques used to transform a person's relationship with food and their body can be effectively applied to various aspects of their life.

This is the message that I hope to convey in this book–that by exploring and transforming your relationship with food, you will learn how to identify and challenge the conditioned habit patterns in other areas of your life and begin to unlock your full potential. Whether you are struggling with disordered eating or simply looking to cultivate a healthier and more fulfilling life, the insights and techniques presented in this book can help you on your journey towards greater wellbeing and growth.

Introduction

Everyone has a relationship with food and eating; it may be good, it may be bad, it may be ugly. Whatever it is, it is unique to each of us, and, like all relationships, it is excruciatingly complex.

The purpose of this book is to help you to develop an intimate understanding of *your* relationship with food and eating. As you read the book, and as you engage in the various exercises and practise the suggested tools, you will uncover how to change your eating habits for the better. You will discover that you have an inner wisdom that can guide you on how to nourish yourself in the healthiest and most loving way. Once you accomplish this, you will no longer have the need to follow diet plans made by others, advice from "experts," or norms set by society. You will simply tap into an intuitive ***knowingness*** of what, how, and when to eat, in a way that best serves *you*.

But that is just the beginning. As you become more aware of your relationship with food and eating, you will learn how to use this awareness as a gateway to understand other aspects of your life. You will see that the thought patterns and behaviours you have regarding food and eating are reflected in many areas of your day-to-day life. These patterns impact your relationships, work, hobbies, successes, and general happiness in ways you're probably completely unaware of. As you become more proficient and trusting of this "knowingness" around food, you will be able to transfer this new wisdom to other situations. As a result, this book will show you that through food and eating, you can make significant and long-lasting changes to your entire life.

The book is split into five parts. In **Part One: The Food Relationship and Weight Loss,** we dive deeply into the relationship between food and eating. We unpack why this relationship is so important, and you will be guided to explore and learn about your own food relationship. Part One also talks about weight loss and the problems that arise when we attempt to force our body to be in a particular weight, shape, or size.

In **Part Two: Rebuilding Your Relationship with Eating**, you will learn a range of techniques that will help you to completely change how you approach food and eating. This will include learning how to listen to your body to tell you when it is hungry or full; discovering that you can trust your body to tell you exactly what it needs; and experiencing the benefits of mindful eating alongside various techniques on how to do it.

In **Part Three: Body Image and Exercise**, we explore the judgements you have about your body and will be presenting strategies to combat these judgements. This part teaches you how to practically change your behaviours related to weight, shape, and size.

In **Part Four: Beyond Food and Eating**, we will extend beyond the realm of nourishment and body image. In this part, you'll witness how your newfound understanding and experiences will ripple into every corner of your life. This part is all about transformation across all aspects of your being.

Finally, **Part Five: Questions and Answers**, covers common questions that come up when people embark on a journey to reform their relationship with food, eating, and their body. This aims to give you a taste of the main stumbling blocks and concerns people have when they start doing this work. By sharing this, I hope that you will see that you are not alone, both in terms of what you are going through and any difficulties you may come across using this approach.

In every chapter you will also find experiential tasks and homework practices to do on your own. It is a good idea to have a dedicated notebook or journal on hand. Be sure to give yourself time and a quiet space to really delve into the tasks. Sometimes, I will suggest a time range for each exercise but unless it specifically states otherwise, please do not feel restricted by that. Some people require more or less depending on the topic and how deep they want to go. Also, please note that not every idea or task presented in this book will resonate with you. You will come to learn that the only person who knows what you need, is you! An array of tried and tested techniques and approaches will be offered but they are just suggestions. **Trust yourself.** Try the various tools; keep hold of those that are the right fit, and let go of anything that doesn't serve you.

All the methods, ideas, case studies, and tasks in this book are the result of years of experience, learnings, and positive outcomes. They stem from psychological theories, evidence-based treatment approaches, anecdotal evidence, wellbeing, and spiritual practices. Most of these methods have been adapted from other sources and are presented in a way that I have found to be accessible to the people I work with. Almost all concepts will have my own spin on them but in the words of Mark Twain:

> *"There is no such thing as a new idea. It is impossible. We simply take a lot of old ideas and put them into a sort of mental kaleidoscope. We give them a turn and they make new and curious combinations. We keep on turning and making new combinations indefinitely; but they are the same old pieces of coloured glass that have been in use through all the ages."*

I hope that the combination I am offering in this book will speak to you in such a way that it supports the life-changing alterations you have been searching for.

Privacy Note:

The case examples you'll find in this book are drawn from real-life situations. However, great care has been taken to ensure the privacy and confidentiality of the individuals involved. To achieve this, alterations have been made to names, locations, and other details, while keeping the heart of these stories intact and maintaining the authenticity of the narratives.

PART I

THE FOOD RELATIONSHIP AND WEIGHT LOSS

"Food is our common ground, a universal experience."

- James Beard

CHAPTER 1:

The importance of food

Food is more than just sustenance; it's the essence of life. Food nourishes us in a way that goes beyond mere survival. Unlike breathing, which happens automatically, food consumption requires making conscious choices. We decide what to eat, when to eat, and how much to eat. We engage in the process of seeking, producing, choosing, and consuming food. Without proper nourishment, daily life becomes a challenge for humans and animals alike. In short, food holds the power to fuel our body, mind, and spirit. Furthermore, in modern society, food is everywhere. Food surrounds us with an immense array of choices and unprecedented availability. Yet, despite this abundance, our relationship with food has reached an all-time low. The very society that is blessed with so much, finds itself grappling with a deteriorating connection to food and the bodies it serves.

- At some point in their lives, approximately one out of every six women and one out of every 10 men in the US will experience an eating disorder. (NEDA, 2022)

- Over one million Brits have an eating disorder, such as anorexia, bulimia, or binge eating. (NHS, 2021)

- Young women aged 15-24 have the highest rate of anorexia, with a 1-year rate of 0.3%. (JAMA Psychiatry, 2019)

- Body Dysmorphic Disorder affects 1-2% of the general population, with even higher rates seen in those seeking cosmetic surgery or with eating disorders. It has a twelvefold increased risk of suicide. (Fang et al., 2016)

- Two-thirds of women and a third of all men state that they feel pressure to "have a perfect body." (American Psychological Association)

- 45% of women and 25% of men engage in unhealthy weight control, such as skipping meals or taking laxatives. (Journal of the Academy of Nutrition and Dietetics, 2021)

- Men are three times as likely as women to exhibit subthreshold Binge Eating Disorder. This means they demonstrate significant disordered eating patterns that don't meet all the criteria for an official diagnosis of Binge Eating Disorder. (Hudson et al, 2007)
- 20% of adults report eating emotionally, e.g. due to stress or other negative emotions. (Journal of Health Psychology, 2019)
- 30% of adolescents report that they restrict their eating or engage in binge eating. (Journal of Adolescent Health, 2021; International Journal of Eating Disorders, 2020)

Clearly the food relationship is not simply just about having access to food and eating. It extends beyond mere nourishment. It encompasses societal standards of "desirable" body shapes, and is impacted by a lack of food education and necessitates navigating food labels correctly. Most importantly, it is impacted when there is a disconnect from our own internal wisdom.

"The table is a meeting
place, a gathering ground,
the source of sustenance and
nourishment, festivity, safety,
and satisfaction."

- **Laurie Colwin**

CHAPTER 2:

How the food relationship is formed

Our connection with food begins to take shape from the earliest stages of life. During the first days, weeks, and months of infancy, the way we are fed has a profound impact on our future food relationships. Extensive research demonstrates that the feeding interactions between caregiver and child play a vital role in fostering secure bonding and attachment. It goes beyond providing nutrition; it involves emotional support, comfort, and nurturing. Studies even suggest that in these early stages, there is a level of awareness that can influence later behaviours. With this in mind, let's explore some common feeding experiences that unfold from birth through the initial weeks and months of development.

> **BITE SIZED THOUGHT**
>
> The examples presented below are not extreme or extenuating circumstances. They simply illustrate some common experiences that have been associated with early feeding difficulties.

From the moment we start feeding a newborn, we can encounter various challenges. Some babies struggle with breastfeeding due to difficulties with latching, leaving them exhausted and unable to get enough milk. Others may face the hurdle of insufficient milk production from their breastfeeding mothers, resulting in inadequate nourishment. Sometimes there may even be medical conditions that impede the child's ability to absorb nutrients, even if they appear to be eating well. These early feeding experiences can leave infants feeling frustrated and deprived. While more research is needed to fully understand the impact, studies suggest that these challenges may unconsciously shape a sense of scarcity or "not enough" within the baby's developing psyche.

Another common occurrence is when new parents adhere to a specific structured routine they have read about or been instructed to follow. When I provide parenting coaching it's not uncommon to hear parents talk about specific feeding and sleeping schedules they follow with their children. However, not all babies adhere to these schedules. Some little ones may protest, leaving their parents desperately searching for ways to soothe them. What these parents may not realise is that their baby's cries could be signalling hunger and the need for more food. Questions like, "How can my baby be hungry if I fed her less than two hours ago?" arise more frequently than one might expect.

There is also a phenomenon that is seldom admitted or discussed. This is when parents unconsciously, or even consciously, limit their babies' food intake due to concerns about weight. This tends to occur more often with slightly older babies and toddlers. It's not a deliberate decision to withhold food; rather, it manifests as a hesitation to offer extra food or encourage additional eating. Subtle comments such as "don't be greedy" might be uttered in such situations. This practice, while less common, can still have a considerable impact on a child's feeding experiences and their relationship with food. The root cause is often the parents' uncertainty about what constitutes a normal or healthy size for a 1- or 2-year-old, leading them to impose restrictions based on their personal perceptions.

Interestingly, there are some babies who quickly adapt to the unpredictability of feeding, accepting that nourishment arrives when it does, regardless of their body's cues. This early acceptance could become their first experience of mistrusting their innate hunger signals. On the other hand, I have observed instances where there is an overreliance on baby formula, driven by the belief that the baby needs additional nourishment. This can happen due to a desire to encourage the baby to sleep through the night, concern about insufficient feeding, or a reaction to early feeding difficulties that have left the parents feeling guilty and attempting to compensate. It is essential to note that this does not imply that infants should not feel full and satisfied after feeding. Rather, it is about recognising that infants possess a natural ability to regulate their own intake and will typically stop eating when they are full. If they appear to want more than what they have been given, offering additional food is reasonable. The problem arises when parents attempt to ensure their baby is well-fed and content but overlook the signs of fullness and disregard the baby's natural cues. Coaxing a baby to eat more after they have indicated fullness can disrupt their innate self-regulation, leading to a mistrust of their own cues and an expectation to feel excessively full with every meal.

Luckily, such experiences on their own unlikely to trigger a life-time of eating, food, and body-related difficulties, but it would be an oversight to write off such early experiences as something that has no influence on later patterns. At the very least, we know that family behaviours tend to repeat themselves. So, the parents who offer a top-up to an already well-fed *baby* are likely to offer a top-up to an already well-fed *child*. It is very possible that the infant's unconscious relationship with food and eating and the corresponding feelings, both physical and emotional, are initiated from a very early age. This certainly appeared to be the case for my client Jacob.

> *Jacob was a 9-year-old boy whose parents brought him to see me for his picky eating. Jacob, though healthy, was very slim for his age and had an extremely limited diet. He was only willing to eat pizza and omelettes, with an*

occasional cheese sandwich thrown in on a good day. His under-eating made his mother extremely worried and, as a result, she would cave to Jacob's daily demands for KitKats, chocolate milk, ice cream and other such snacks. Of course, this created a vicious cycle in which the snacks filled Jacob, so he was no longer hungry for his food when meal time came around. It was clear to Jacob's parents that this cycle of snacks was worsening his likelihood of eating other foods, but during the times when they had tried to remove the snacks, Jacob would cry inconsolably. He would scream as though he hadn't eaten in weeks, claim he was starving, and beg his parents for the candy. The severity of Jacob's cries undoubtedly resulted in his parents reverting back to the snacks.

As part of my work with the family, I observed Jacob during some of these outbursts. He did get into a state of panic when his snacks were not given. His presentation seemed as though he felt he would literally starve if he didn't get the candy. At times, he would get so worked up that he would even make himself sick.

Having worked with many families with picky-eating children, I knew it was very important to go through Jacob's history from when he was a baby. Unsurprisingly, he had a significant postnatal history. Jacob was born with a condition called esophageal atresia in which his oesophagus (food pipe) was not correctly connected to his stomach. His condition was not diagnosed right away, which meant that Jacob was unknowingly struggling to swallow and digest his milk correctly. During this time he was inconsolable, screaming and quite literally starving, without anyone knowing what was going on. Once the condition was diagnosed, Jacob had a small surgery and the issue was fixed. There were no more physical issues, but his mother was left with an excruciating guilt for not having realised the issue sooner. She said she had night-mares about his screams as a baby for weeks after the surgery and had experienced postnatal depression triggered by the events. She explained that the experience had meant that as Jacob started eating solids, she would give him whatever he wanted. Before long, Jacob was a toddler and demanded snacks. He was choosing to eat these snacks over the other foods his parents offered him. When he didn't get the snacks, he would scream in such a way that it seemed he was reliving the period of time when he was a baby and not able to get the food he needed. His screams then triggered his mom's guilt, and the process was perpetuated. It would seem that Jacob's experiences as a baby stayed with him and his mom, and they were still manifesting in a similar way after all these years.

BITE SIZED THOUGHT

Are you aware of stories about you from when you were a baby? Did you have any trouble with feeding? Were there any difficulties that you or your caregivers experienced that may have impacted your feeding? If you have no idea, it might be good to speak to your parents, siblings, or other caregivers that were around during that time in case they remember anything. Learning about your early feeding experiences is useful for understanding the very early food and eating relationships you developed. If you're not in touch with family, they've passed away, or you've checked and found no problems, don't worry. While valuable, this information isn't pivotal to grasping the development of your food and eating dynamic.

As children grow, they gain more control over their food choices. At this time, they also start to absorb beliefs and opinions expressed by the closest people around them, like their family and friends. Exposure to these ideas has a powerful impact on how they start to think and behave themselves. Consequently, certain traits and habit patterns start to develop. While of course we know that genetics and unique predispositions play a role, research shows that our surroundings, including social and cultural factors, greatly influence the persona that develops later in life. This understanding emphasises the significant inter-play between our innate tendencies and the world around us in shaping our thoughts, actions, and personal characteristics. So, if children repeatedly hear negative comments about having a larger body size, they are likely to internalise the belief that being bigger is undesirable. Consequently, they may develop a desire to engage in activities that help them avoid weight gain or maintain a smaller body size. Similarly, children who witness people cutting out entire food groups or following restrictive diets may perceive these behaviours as the "right" way to eat. They might adopt similar practices, thinking that eliminating certain foods is necessary for health or appearance. The more they keep acting on these beliefs, the more those beliefs and their corresponding behaviours get stronger, becoming even more solid in their minds. Without any awareness of this happening, these patterns of beliefs and behaviours become habitual and, over time, shape their perception of who they believe they are, which can stick with them throughout their whole lives. For example consider a scenario where a 4-year-old girl witnesses her mother counting calories, scrutinising herself in the mirror, and struggling with food. In such a situation, the child is likely to internalise these actions as normal and potentially develop a lasting belief that these behaviours are the standard way to relate to food and one's body.

It is important to recognise that we do have the ability to challenge and transform these patterns. This realisation is empowering because it means that our current thoughts and actions do not define who we truly are. In fact, this is a positive aspect because if our thoughts and behaviours were fixed and unchangeable there would be no point in trying to improve ourselves! Nothing would work; making an effort wouldn't change anything, going to therapy would be of no use, there would even be no point in reading this book! But because we can and do change, it means our thoughts, beliefs, feelings, and even behaviours (including the "bad" ones) are not who we are. Nonetheless, in order to make these changes, we first need to become aware of them. This is the critical first step. As we begin to contemplate the events and stories that have shaped our current relationship with food and our bodies, we open ourselves up to gaining valuable insights into the influences, conditioning, and patterns of thinking, feeling, and behaving that have contributed to our present state. Armed with this newfound understanding, we can then embark on a journey of positive change.

BITE SIZED THOUGHT

The interplay between experiences, behaviours, and the formation of belief systems is an underpinning element of various psychological treatments. Approaches like Cognitive-Behavioral Therapy (CBT), Schema Therapy, Rational Emotive Behavior Therapy (REBT), Transactional Analysis (TA), Social Cognitive Theory (SCT), Experiential Therapy (ET), and others, all recognise the profound impact of these dynamics and consider them as the fundamental building blocks of their respective models. Consequently, addressing and understanding these patterns are essential aspects of psychological therapy, forming the bedrock upon which its effectiveness in assisting individuals is built.

CHAPTER 3:

The influence of childhood beliefs on adult eating habits

Through my years supporting clients with their eating difficulties, I've encountered various beliefs about food that originate in childhood and profoundly influence behaviours later in life. There are several common themes that consistently impact the development of food, eating, and body difficulties as individuals grow older.

One prevalent theme is the requirement to finish everything on the plate, often accompanied by references to starving children in other parts of the world. Hearing this message repeatedly can lead to a lifelong habit of being a member of the "clean plate club," where one feels compelled to eat everything in front of them regardless of fullness. Another common scenario involves one child feeling the need to eat quickly to keep up with their siblings. They often report that this rushed mindless eating habit will then persist into adulthood.

Yet another significant theme arises when a child witnesses a parent criticising their own body and restricting certain food groups as part of a diet. This sends a clear message that our bodies are something to dislike, and that avoiding specific foods is necessary for feeling better.

Lastly, in more severe cases, children may experience heartbreaking situations such as starvation, humiliation, or abuse related to food, eating, or their body. These events have a profound and excruciatingly painful impact on those who endure them.

It doesn't always matter how subtle or traumatic these experiences were, nor does the original intention matter. The experience alone contributes to the relationship that develops over time and, in many cases, the result is a life-long battle of self-loathing, distrust, uncertainty, or confusion about food, eating, and the body. Sometimes, the memories or associations may even appear positive on the surface, but they can still lead to negative outcomes like attachment, dependence, or a form of conditional love, as was illustrated by my client, Clarita.

Clarita was a 26-year-old woman who sought help for her eating issues. She expressed her struggle with turning to food during fraught times, and engaging in emotional overeating. Initially, she believed her lack of willpower was to blame and attempted to compensate for her eating behaviours through diets and excessive exercise. Despite her efforts, she felt like a failure and hoped I could provide strategies to become a "better dieter."

Right from the start, I made it clear that I couldn't assist her in becoming a better dieter. Instead, I offered to work with her to understand her relationship with food and eating, guiding her toward making positive changes in her life.

Clarita and I delved into her childhood experiences with food, where a significant theme emerged–her frequent visits to her grandma's house. She described her grandmother as a caring, sweet, and kind person who was also an excellent baker. During those visits, she was constantly treated to delectable homemade cakes and indulgent hot cocoa, accompanied by her grandmother's warmth, love, and kindness. Her grandma often used phrases like "here's some apple pie for being a special little girl" or "sweet lovely girls get grandma's delicious pudding."

Unbeknownst to Clarita, this led her to develop unconscious associations between eating specific foods, particularly deliciously sweet baked goods, and feeling special and loved. Interestingly, by exploring her eating behaviours she discovered that during highly stressful times her appetite would actually diminish, so she realised that her overeating was specifically related to feeling unloved or "lacking in specialness," as she described it.

She recalled a time when her boyfriend broke up with her, and she immediately drove to a donut shop and devoured five large donuts. Similarly, she recounted a birthday cele-

*bration gone awry when her friend cancelled at the last
minute. Feeling lonely and uncared for, Clarita went to
the store and purchased a large cake. Through tears, she
sang herself happy birthday and consumed almost the
entire cake alone.*

*Clarita's overeating wasn't a result of a lack of willpower.
Dieting and restricting were unintended consequences that
exacerbated the issue. The root cause was her belief that
consuming these foods made her feel special and loved.*

*Once Clarita realised that her struggle wasn't solely about
the food itself but rather how she related to it, she began
to make significant changes. She focused on building her
self-esteem and learned that she didn't require anything or
anyone to make her feel special and loved. Importantly,
during challenging moments when she was on the verge
of reaching for the cake, she fully understood why she was
doing it. Sometimes, this awareness alone empowered her
to resist the temptation. Other times, she indulged in the
cake, but with a complete awareness of her motivations. As
a result, a single generous slice was often enough.*

The lessons Clarita gained pave the way for the next chapter:
the power of understanding our past behaviours, in order to
shape a more empowered future.

CHAPTER 4:

The best predictor of future behaviour is past behaviour

We've all heard the saying, "history repeats itself." In many cases, that's true. Our past actions, thoughts, and experiences often shape the way we act, think, and approach life. This holds particularly true for behaviours that are consistently and persistently expressed over time. Interestingly, there's evidence that this impact is unique not only to one's behaviours, but also to thought patterns and feelings. It is for this reason that it is important to explore our past history. By examining the thoughts, feelings, and behaviours that have evolved over the years, beginning in childhood, we gain deeper insight into the origins of our current food and eating relationships, as well as the influential factors that have strengthened these patterns.

So now it's your turn to investigate! By exploring your childhood experiences, you may be able to start to uncover some of your core beliefs. This is often the first channel to learn about your relationship with food and eating.

LET'S GET WORKING:
Exploring Your Childhood History

INSTRUCTIONS: For this exercise, you'll need your journal.

⏳ *15 - 20 minutes*

This exercise encourages you to revisit memories, beliefs, and events related to food from your past. You're welcome to write about positive or negative experiences.

You can choose to focus on specific events or beliefs, or create a list of various lessons you learned about food during your childhood.

To help guide you, consider the prompts below:

Family Meal Times:
- Did your family regularly eat meals together during your childhood?
- How did these shared meals make you feel?
- What specific memories stand out from those times?

Memorable Eating Experiences:
- Can you recall any significant eating experiences from your childhood?

- How did these experiences leave an impact on you?
- Describe the emotions attached to these memories, whether they were related to trying new foods, family gatherings, or other events involving food.

Influential Beliefs:
- Reflect on the messages or beliefs about food that you encountered while growing up.
- Where did these beliefs come from? (Family, culture, personal experiences)
- How do you believe these beliefs have shaped your relationship with food as you've grown older?

Open your journal and dedicate at least five minutes to delving into your childhood memories and emotions regarding your food and eating journey. Write freely about the experiences that come to mind.

Happy writing!

By doing the exercise above, you may have identified some key events, messages, experiences, and beliefs from your childhood that play a big part in how you relate to food and eating in your life.

Once we gain an understanding about how our issues with food and eating developed, it can stir up intense emotions like anger, resentment, or the inclination to blame those who may have influenced our experiences. Whether these negative associations arise from friends, family, or a broader societal or cultural context that propagated unhelpful and harmful messages about what, when, and how to eat, it's crucial to keep the following statement in mind:

> *My relationship with food has served a purpose in my life exactly as it needed to. I needed to undergo these experiences in order to gain clarity about myself and undergo personal growth. There's no need to harbour hatred towards the individuals or circumstances that contributed to this relationship, even if I believe these experiences to be deeply traumatic and distressing.*
>
> *My relationship with food is not fixed; it is dynamic and can be transformed. I am currently putting in the effort to bring about this change.*

Read these words multiple times to allow their meaning to sink in.

After engaging in the journaling exercise, you may have uncovered some things that you were already aware of, or maybe you gained valuable clarity about the origins of your current behaviours. It's also possible that nothing significant came to mind. Perhaps you recalled overwhelmingly positive events from your past that don't align with your current relationship with food and eating. Rest assured, you are not alone in this!

I've come across numerous cases where childhood experiences were incredibly nurturing. Families would lovingly gather around the table, free from distractions. They would serve delicious and wholesome food and encourage the exploration and enjoyment of different tastes. There was an understanding that it's okay to savour what you eat and leave behind what you don't want to finish. Moreover, there was a genuine appreciation for the body. Yet, even amidst these regular positive familial experiences, it didn't always guarantee immunity from disordered eating and a negative body image.

When it comes to beliefs about food and eating, even with a foundation of positive experiences, you still have to contend with societal pressures, cultural fixations, nutritional misinformation, and conflicting advice. Body ideals are constantly shifting. What's considered desirable in one era may not be in another. Fat, carbs, sugars – the enemy changes with passing fashions. And let's not forget the cultural differences: While some cultures celebrate curves, others worship thinness. The truth is, the world of food, eating, and body image can be a simmering pot of fear-driven madness. Even those with the strongest foundations can be pulled into this spiral.

Thankfully, it isn't all doom and gloom. There are indeed individuals who naturally remain unaffected by the unhelpful associations that come their way. They may be aware of the challenges that others face and are exposed to the same overwhelming information on the subject. Yet, they either possess a strong sense of self-acceptance or simply remain unfazed by it all. This could be attributed to their internal resilience or, their own personal disposition that shields them from responding to external cues in the same detrimental manner as others.

Then there are those who have suffered, sometimes for much of their life, and come to the decision that they want to do something about it. These individuals may either start to work on themselves by themselves, or they reach out for help. This is often the case for the people who meet with me at a seminar, workshop, retreat, or for one-to-one work. Over time and with the right tools and support, they are able to transform their negative relationships and shift from fear, hate, and disgust–to that of acceptance, love, and joy. This again illustrates that with awareness and effort, transformation is possible.

I hope you're beginning to understand that **everyone has a unique connection with food and eating**, whether it's a positive or challenging one. This connection is shaped by a multitude of experiences throughout our lives. It's a complex relationship, but just like any other relationship, it is not set in stone and can be transformed. The more we become aware of this relationship, the greater the opportunity we have for significant change.

CHAPTER 5:

Your food and eating relationship today

Now that you have gained awareness about the development of your food relationship, it's time to examine your connection to food and eating today. We will do so by taking a broader look at the messages, ideas, beliefs, and experiences you currently hold regarding food and eating. These encompass the rich tapestry of thoughts you've internalised about nourishment.

For instance, you may have absorbed notions like "I must endure a 14-hour gap between my evening meal and breakfast the next day."

Or perhaps you've encountered prevailing food-related statements such as "carbs are the enemy," "sugar is poison," or "I just look at a piece of bread and my thighs get fat."

Even if you believe you have no issues and generally feel content with your relationship to food; even if you think you already possess a firm grasp on the subject and have perhaps spent considerable time in therapy unravelling its complexities–I implore you to revisit it once more. Every time we dive into self-exploration, we may unveil something new. Sometimes, a subtle shift in phrasing can spark a fresh perspective, causing us to reassess what we thought we understood about ourselves.

This was illustrated by my client, Melanie.

Melanie, a 30-year-old personal trainer who also had a strong interest in food and eating, was attending a health and wellbeing event where I was giving a talk. She saw that I was going to be discussing "how to transform your relationship with food, eating, and your body" and decided to come and listen. After the workshop, Melanie approached me, her expression filled with surprise and introspection. She admitted that before my talk she believed she had complete control over her food choices and felt confident about her body. She considered her intense exercise routine and restricted eating habits to be crucial for maintaining a "healthy lifestyle." Initially, she didn't expect to learn anything new and revealed that she attended the session mainly because she had some free time and hoped to gain advice to share with her struggling clients. However, something I said during the talk struck a chord with her and made her question her beliefs. The statement was this: **"People who have a healthy relationship with food rarely think about it, unless they are eating. People** *with an unhealthy relationship think about food all the time, except when they are eating."*

This is a statement that is widely utilised by professionals who are working with clients to develop healthy relationships with food. It resonated deeply with Melanie and, according to her, left her stunned.

The reality hit her when she realised how many hours each day were consumed by her obsessive thoughts about food. Although she had convinced herself that it was justified as part of her job, taking a closer look made her realise that this excuse was far from valid. Just as I had mentioned, she discovered that she spent an excessive amount of time preparing, planning, and fixating on food. In the midst of her busy schedule, she barely allowed herself the luxury of sitting down and truly savouring her meals. Instead, she would hurriedly devour food while driving between clients or mindlessly eat in front of the TV to unwind after a long day. She became acutely aware of the countless hours she spent scouring the internet for food and diet advice, while neglecting to truly listen to her own body's needs. She confessed to eliminating various food groups, even claiming intolerances without ever genuinely observing how her body reacted to the foods she restricted.

Melanie stated that she felt overwhelmed. She said she thought she knew how she related to food and eating, but now realised she actually knew a lot about what other people think on the matter and was relatively unaware of her own stance. Inspired to embark on a transformative journey, she began working with me to explore and reshape her relationship with food.

Now, the spotlight shifts to you as we embark on a journey to uncover your present-day thoughts and beliefs surrounding food. It's time to reflect on your current relationship with food and delve into the ideas that shape your eating choices and habits.

LET'S GET WORKING:
Exploring Your Relationship with Food and Eating

INSTRUCTIONS: For this exercise, you'll need your journal.

⏳ *15 - 20 minutes*

This exercise encourages you to delve into your current beliefs, thoughts, behaviours, and emotions surrounding food and eating. Just like the previous exercise, feel free to be as detailed as you wish, and take guidance from the prompts provided below.

What are your food and eating rules?
• Do you eliminate specific food groups?
• Do you categorise certain foods as 'good' or 'bad?'
• Are you following a specific diet plan?

How does your eating behaviour change based on external circumstances?
• Do you notice shifts in your eating habits on bad days?
• Does the presentation of food influence your choices?

- Do gestures like someone preparing food specially impact your eating?

Examine your physical and emotional feelings when consuming foods you negatively judge:
- Do certain foods make you feel a particular way, physically and emotionally?
- How do you cope with eating foods that trigger negative judgments?
- Do you resort to restricting intake, extreme diets, purging, or using laxative teas?

Reflect on your thoughts after a 'bad' eating day:
- What thoughts arise when you believe you haven't had a good eating day?

Identify the factors influencing your beliefs, thoughts, behaviours, and comments related to food and eating:
- Are there specific comments from others that shape your views?
- Do advice or articles impact your food choices?
- Are societal pressures influencing your eating habits?
- How does so-called 'scientific' evidence affect your decisions?

Take this time to introspect and jot down your thoughts honestly. Use the provided prompts to guide your exploration

Happy writing!

By now, you hopefully have deepened your understanding of your relationship with food and eating. Perhaps you recognise more clearly the constant mental chatter surrounding food and the specific thoughts and emotions that accompany every act of eating.

On the other hand, you may have made the intriguing discovery that food and eating hold little significance in your life. You find yourself operating on "auto-pilot," guided by external factors like clock time, portion sizes, and the preferences of others. This realisation is just as fascinating–a recognition of being disconnected from the fundamental sustenance of life. But even if you fall into the rare category of individuals who genuinely have a positive relationship with food, I encourage you to continue reading. Why? Because this book still holds relevance for you. As you identify the automatic thoughts and behavioural patterns that contribute to your healthy relationship with food, you'll come to understand that it doesn't have to end there. With heightened awareness, you open yourself up to something truly extraordinary–a gateway that transcends the boundaries of mere food and eating. Whatever you have learnt so far, you'll soon discover how your specific relationship with food can become a catalyst for transforming every aspect of your life.

CHAPTER 6:

When weight loss is your goal

I'll never forget this moment at a friend's birthday party:

A tap on my shoulder caught my attention. As I turned around, I saw a vaguely familiar face–it was Sharri, a high school acquaintance I hadn't seen in years. We exchanged greetings, started chatting and I soon understood that she knew very little about my adult life or my occupation. However, our conversation was abruptly interrupted as the lights dimmed and the crowd burst into a lively rendition of "Happy Birthday" for the birthday girl. After blowing out the candles, the cake was passed around. Sharri eagerly accepted a generous slice.

As I observed the cake making its way to me, I paused to assess my own desires. Having enjoyed a satisfying dinner before the party, the cake didn't particularly entice me, so

I gracefully declined a slice. Sharri, noticing my choice, glanced at me from head to toe and remarked.

"Oh, are you on a diet?"

As if that was the only possible reason for turning down cake.

"No," I replied. "I just don't feel like having cake right now."

Her eyes widened, and she responded, "Wow, if I could resist cake just because I didn't feel like it, I'd be so much thinner."

Her words trailed off as she once again scanned my appearance.

Almost everyone I meet tells me they want to change their relationship with food. Yet, immediately after they say this, it is usually followed with, "because, if I had a better relationship with food, I would be able to lose weight." It's important to recognise that **wanting to lose weight is not the same as wanting to change your relationship with food**. When weight loss, or more specifically, altering your body's appearance, becomes the sole focus, it sends a message: "I am not good enough as I am. I need to be different." This thought isn't rooted in love or self-acceptance; it stems from fear. It's the fear that we are inherently inadequate. When we hold this belief to be true, our behaviours align with it. We may resort to undereating, restricting food, engaging in extreme dieting practices, and more. After all, if we view ourselves negatively and doubt our own worth, how can we trust ourselves to nourish our bodies properly? It becomes easier to punish ourselves by withholding the food our body truly needs—even when it cries out for sustenance. Paradoxically, these fear-driven behaviours only reinforce our self-destructive beliefs. The more we resist our body's natural cues, restrict our food intake, and chase after weight loss, the more challenging it becomes. Ultimately, we find ourselves falling short, which further confirms our deep-rooted belief that we are not good enough and that we cannot trust our bodies.

BITE SIZED
THOUGHT

Often, when I tell clients the idea of a loving approach to eating–one with self-acceptance and kindness–I get all sorts of responses. Some say, "I am overweight," "I'm obese," or "I have a medical condition because of my eating habits; how can I trust myself to eat when I let this happen to myself?" Others exclaim, "I am way too easy on myself! I just let myself eat everything and anything. I need more self-control when it comes to food! How can you tell me to be *more* loving and accepting?" Then there are those who say, "It's good to be afraid of food and wanting to diet and control what I eat. When I was younger, I got bullied for being overweight, and it really hurt. The only way I can keep the weight off is by dieting and strictly controlling what I eat."

Treating yourself with kindness doesn't mean you can't also make significant changes to how you approach, choose, and eat your food. It's just that your focus shifts to your health and wellbeing. It's about making positive changes in your life rather than obsessing over your weight or appearance.

Changing your relationship with food, eating, and your body places a different emphasis altogether. It begins with the acknowledgement that **you are inherently worthy**. From this place of self-acceptance and love, your approach to nourishing your body should reflect this profound understanding. It's not about trying to change who you are, but rather about discovering what truly serves you in the most optimal way. This shift in mindset is more than just a matter of semantics–it's crucial.

When the focus is solely on weight loss, your choices become centred around how your body might appear, rather than what your body truly needs. As a result, it becomes difficult to foster an authentic and loving relationship with food and your body. The intention behind changing your relationship is rooted in embracing your inherent worthiness, prioritising self-care, and making choices that honour and nourish your body from a place of love.

The following examples show the difference between someone who is acting out fear-based eating versus love-based eating.

Fear-based eating

It's 11:30 a.m., and though your stomach grumbles with hunger, you resist the urge to eat until it's officially "lunch time."

After what feels like an eternity, you finally pull out your pre-made salad bowl. Disappointment sets in as you look down: just a few plain vegetables and some lean protein with a tasteless, low-calorie dressing. You hurriedly consume it, hoping it will stave off the hunger, but it leaves you feeling physically unsatisfied and still craving something more.

Today, you're driven by a mixture of fear–either fear of gaining weight or fear of straying from your strict diet plan. But your motivation starts to waver when you take a lunchtime walk and pass by a delightful bakery. The mouth-watering cookies and cupcakes beckon you like sirens calling a sailor to the rocks. You can't help but glance longingly at them, torn between your desire to indulge and the commitment to stick to your diet.

Just as you're trying to convince yourself to walk away, a friendly woman from the bakery approaches, offering samples. The aroma of freshly baked goodness fills the air, and you can practically taste the sweetness on your tongue. Temptation takes hold, and you try one of the cookies. It's a burst of delight, but the guilt immediately washes over you like a tidal wave.

Struggling to resist further, you somehow manage to walk away and continue your stroll, but you can't stop thinking about those delectable treats. The internal battle rages within you–the desire to enjoy something sweet versus the fear of failing your diet. Eventually, the struggle proves too much to bear. You cave in to the powerful cravings, deciding to buy both a cookie and a doughnut, promising yourself you'll share one with someone else to alleviate the guilt.

Yet, before you even leave the store, you break off a piece of the cookie and devour it hastily, feeling a mix of pleasure and self-reproach with each bite. As the cookie disappears rapidly, you turn to the doughnut, thinking, "I've already messed up my diet today, I may as well eat this one too" You devour it as well, quickly, without savouring the taste, just trying to escape the grip of temptation.

Standing alone in an alley, you feel the weight of shame and disappointment, berating yourself for lacking self-control. "What have I done?" you think. "I am pathetic, gross, and out of control." You feel mad at yourself, vowing to start fresh tomorrow. But the cycle of fear-based eating seems never-ending, leaving you feeling defeated and helpless.

Love-based eating

It's 11:30 a.m., and you notice your stomach rumbling. Hunger prompts you to consider lunch and, honouring your body's needs, you decide to have it a little bit early. On this warm day, you opt for a visit to a lovely café. The menu offers a mouthwatering salad bowl, filled with an array of colourful, fresh vegetables, a choice of delectable protein and a generous sprinkling of seeds and nuts on top. And to enhance the flavour, a rich and delicious dressing is served on the side.

As you take your first bite, you relish the variety of tastes and textures dancing on your palate. The dressing complements the salad beautifully, and you skillfully mix it in, just enough to coat the ingredients evenly. Eating becomes an experience of enjoyment and mindfulness as you savour each bite with appreciation.

This dish is large. About three-quarters of your way through you become aware of your body's signals. You're feeling content and notice that you're getting full. Instead of forcing yourself to finish, you kindly request the café staff to pack the remaining portion for later, knowing you can enjoy this delicious meal again when hunger strikes.

Continuing your day, you pass by a bakery, and a friendly lady offers samples of their delightful treats. Curious and open to indulging in a moment of sweetness, you decide to try one. Savouring the flavour, you take another sample and thoughtfully put it in your takeaway box for a later treat when you desire something sweet. You make a mental note to revisit this charming store next time you feel like baked goods.

With a sense of balance and self-compassion, you carry on with your day, nourishing your body with love-based eating. Your food choices are no longer driven by fear or strict diets, but rather by the genuine enjoyment of nourishing yourself and treating yourself with kindness.

These two examples paint a vivid contrast between the ways we engage with food–either driven by fear or guided by love. Fear-based eating reveals the inner turmoil of denying oneself and then succumbing to temptation, a cycle that breeds dissatisfaction and self-reproach. In stark juxtaposition, love-based eating showcases the art of savouring each bite, respecting body cues, and relishing both nourishment and indulgence without guilt. Through these stories, we come to appreciate that food isn't just sustenance; it's a reflection of our emotions, our relationships with ourselves, and the values we uphold. The choices we make around food can either perpetuate a cycle of negativity or foster a harmonious connection with our bodies. Ultimately, whether we choose fear or love, the stories remind us that every meal is an opportunity to nurture not only our physical wellbeing but also our sense of self-worth and contentment.

Are you really, honestly, acting out of love?

Sometimes, our fear-based actions disguise themselves as loving. This was the case for Austin, a 31-year-old man who came to see me.

During our initial assessment, Austin told me of the many years he had spent dieting, with experiences of self-loathing and struggling with his eating and body image. He described hating his body and said he would punish it for being so gross by restricting foods. Consequently, he would then have periods of overeating until he would vomit. Austin also admitted that alongside wanting to work with me, he was also starting to see a personal trainer who had a qualification in nutrition and was offering a three-month eating program, based largely on the principles of intermittent fasting.

I highlighted the concept of fear-based eating versus love-based eating to Austin and I discussed how it would benefit him to work on changing his relationship to food and eating. I suggested that rather than taking the time now to go on another diet, perhaps he would like to learn how to listen to his body and stop all the dieting behaviours. But before I could even finish what I was saying,

Austin interrupted. He started to recite all the "evidence" in support of intermittent fasting. He told me that it is more important that he give his digestive system a break for great lengths of time, rather than listen to his body, and that his body would learn to adjust. He said that intermittent fasting is the most loving thing he could do for his body. He argued that if he listened to his body, he would simply eat non-stop.

Once Austin finished, I told him that it would be better if he completed his work with his personal trainer. If he ever wanted a different approach, he could come back to me at a later time.

My goal was not to convince Austin that he was actually choosing to relate to food from a fear-based perspective. I also don't fundamentally have any issues with intermittent fasting techniques, if that is a lifestyle preference. The issue here was that despite reporting self-loathing, guilt, and an inability to trust himself, Austin, plagued by his disordered eating, managed to convince himself that his intentions were coming from a place of kindness and self-care. He was ignoring all those feelings of worthlessness, and deluded himself to believe that his driving force was self-care and kindness.

When I encounter individuals like Austin, who genuinely believe they are acting out of love, even though it seems evident to me that their minds may be deceiving them, I refrain from pushing them to see things differently. Over time, I've learned not to rush the process. People will be ready when they're ready. My hope is that I can at least sow a seed of a different perspective in their minds. So, when the time is right and they become aware of their harmful behaviours, they'll have some idea on how to initiate positive changes.

I share this because you might be reading this and recognise someone you know who's acting with misguided intentions. If that's the case, it's alright to share what you've learned with them. However, trying to forcefully impose your perspective when they're not ready is often not a helpful strategy.

The best way to know whether you are truly doing something out of love for your health rather than out of fear is to ask yourself this question:

> **"If my health improved, would I continue to do this even if it made me gain weight?"**

If the answer is "no, I would not do [intermittent fasting, count calories, restrict huge food groups, excessively exercise, etc.] if it caused me to gain weight, even if it was good for my health," then you can be pretty sure you are acting out of fear rather than love. Sometimes, we like to believe we would act differently, but when it actually comes down to it, our body-image obsessions can take over everything else. This was sadly the case for Alexis, a lovely lady I knew and cared deeply about:

> *Alexis was a self-confessed fitness fanatic with a severe eating disorder that she largely downplayed and would not openly admit to (even to herself). Shortly after her 53rd birthday she was diagnosed with a serious cancer and started treatment. One of her medicines caused her to gain quite a bit of weight. In the midst of tremendous suffering, illness and pain, she decided to stop taking the medicine because, in her own words, "I would rather die skinny than be fat."*

LET'S GET WORKING:
Exploring Your Fear-based Eating Experiences

INSTRUCTIONS: For this exercise, you'll need your journal.

⏳ *10 - 15 minutes*

This exercise invites you to explore moments when you may have restricted or altered your eating patterns due to fear of body image or external judgments.

Consider the impact of these choices, whether they brought short-term relief or long-term discomfort, and what has transpired since.

The prompts below can help to guide you.

- Have you ever restricted your food for fear of getting fat?
- Can you recall restricting and binge eating because you didn't feel good enough?
- Did you ever go on a diet just because someone commented on your weight?
- Would you change your eating patterns to try and lose weight for a specific event?

You could choose to focus on one particular time, a few different times, or, if much of your life has been fear-based eating, then perhaps you could draw out some clear themes.

- What did you learn from these eating experiences?

- Was there short-term gain or was it miserable the whole time?
- What happened (or is still happening) after?

Reminder: Fear-based eating comes from believing we are not good enough, so we choose to eat in a way that supports this belief.

Now that we've delved into the factors influencing your behaviours, it's time to be truly honest with yourself about your intentions. If your desire is to transform your relationship with food and eating, paving the way for a life of liberation, freedom, health, and fulfilment, then you've come to the perfect place. However, if your primary focus revolves around losing weight, I must admit that this book may not be for you. Nevertheless, since you've already come this far, I strongly urge you to keep reading. The upcoming section will shed light on the limitations of diets and their transient nature and has the potential to challenge your current ideas, and lead you to reconsider your approach.

CHAPTER 7:

Why diets don't work

Before delving into the issues with diets, let's first clarify what we mean by a "diet." This is especially important because, in recent years, the concept of dieting has gained a negative reputation, prompting the multi-billion dollar diet industry to get crafty. What was once known as a 'diet' is now cleverly marketed as "healthy eating", "clean eating", "detox", and other various buzzwords related to wellness. However, the underlying message remains unchanged: "Do something in order to alter your appearance" - accompanied by some other health-related catchphrases.

My definition of a diet is as follows:

> **"Anything that requires you to exert control, manipulate, or change what, when, and how you eat, with the primary intention of losing weight or altering your body shape."**

BITE SIZED
THOUGHT

It's important to understand that this definition of diets can include both formal diet plans that come from external sources, as well as personal self-directed diets that are based on an individual's own set of rules. I highlight this because some people might not see themselves as traditional dieters, yet they do acknowledge they have an unhealthy relationship with food. On the other hand, chronic dieters might not recognise their eating habits as problematic because they think they're just following a "normal" diet plan that is recommended, such as a low carb/high protein diet. However, both groups often share irrational perceptions, obsessive behaviours, and an excessive focus on their weight, shape, and size. In this book, when I mention a 'dieter,' I'm referring to anyone who fits this description.

Numerous scientific studies have reported that only a small percentage of individuals who attempt weight loss are able to maintain their weight loss in the long term. In fact, it is commonly seen that within three to five years, most people regain a significant portion of the weight they had lost, and sometimes gain even more. Many of my clients, who have been chronic dieters, come to me because the diets they've relied on for so long no longer work. They struggle to lose any weight, and, regardless of their efforts, the numbers on the scale keep going up. Perhaps you find yourself in a similar situation, feeling lost in the cycle of guilt, shame, and inadequacy as an active dieter. You might believe that if you just had more willpower, you'd be successful. But the truth is much more complex than that.

Our ability to lose weight and maintain it involves far more than just sheer willpower or dedication. Some people can persist through torment to achieve their target weight, or they effortlessly overhaul their entire lifestyle. However, for most, the journey is fraught with guilt, shame, inadequacy, and a lower quality of life. The reason behind this struggle isn't laziness or a lack of willpower. In fact, what neuropsychology is revealing is that much of it boils down to how our brains work.

In our brain, there's a special area called the hypothalamus. It is located above the brainstem and plays a vital role in regulating various body functions, including our weight. It takes care of hunger, appetite, metabolism, and more. To understand how the hypothalamus works, we first need to talk about the concept of a set point. In most cases, unless there's a specific medical condition, our bodies have a natural, happy, and healthy weight and size. Just like people have different heights or eye colours, everyone's body tends to stabilise at a healthy, normal weight if left undisturbed. This "set point" isn't an exact number, more like a range of about 10-15 lbs (5-8 kg). For example, if you currently weigh 145 lbs (65kg), your set point might be somewhere between 137-153 lbs (62-68 kg). When your weight changes within this range, it's often due to your lifestyle choices. For example, if you become more active or start to eat more whole foods instead of take-aways, you might see your weight go down. On the other hand, if you start a new job with long hours sitting in front of a computer and not moving much, your weight may go up a little. These are natural, healthy fluctuations that can change a little through simple lifestyle and nutritional changes.

However, the problem starts when our desired weight doesn't match our body's natural set point. Let's say that I weigh 160lbs (72kgs) but I decide I want my weight to be 140lbs (63kg) in that case I might resort to more extreme measures, like significantly changing my food intake (i.e., dieting) or engaging in excessive behaviours (over-exercising, using laxatives, vomiting food, etc.) That's when the hypothalamus comes into play. It acts like a thermostat, switching on when there's not enough food to maintain our body's natural healthy weight. The hypothalamus doesn't know I'm trying to lose weight for bikini season; rather it interprets the situation as a threat. From the hyopthalamus's perspective, the restriction of food is seen as a potential famine where the body might starve.

BITE SIZED
THOUGHT

As frustrating as this may seem to those actively looking to lose weight, this mechanism is actually a
beautiful example of how our bodies are designed to
help us survive. There have been longer periods of
scarcity in our evolutionary journey than there have
been of abundance. Our brain has adapted to ensure
we continue to live in times of famine. Instead of
resenting your body for not resembling an Instagram
model's photoshopped image, perhaps we could show
gratitude to our bodies for their remarkable ability to
ensure our survival.

When your weight dips below its comfortable set point, the
hypothalamus reacts in various ways. It sends signals to your
body's systems, making you feel hungrier, urging your muscles
to burn less energy or store more fat, and so on. Studies suggest
that losing around 10% of your body weight could lead to
burning up to 400 calories less due to a slower metabolism.
This is equivalent to skipping a whole meal. In order to maintain their lower weight, dieters may need to eat one meal less
than those whose set point naturally aligns with that lower
weight.

This restriction process not only triggers the metabolic changes
mentioned earlier, but it can also cause the hypothalamus to

raise the set point. Once you stop restricting and return to regular eating, your "normal" weight becomes higher than when you started. From an evolutionary perspective, this makes sense as your body might believe "times of famine" are frequent, encouraging you to carry more weight to prepare for such periods.

Importantly, research shows that while set points can increase with ease, it is more challenging to lower one's set point. Even after successfully maintaining your lower weight for seven years, your brain will persistently push you to regain it. Conversely, if you gain weight during breaks from dieting or due to overeating, your brain might consider this your new normal. If you imagine that this happens with each diet attempt, it's no wonder many chronic dieters state that they wish they could go back to the weight they had been when they first started dieting. I often hear from clients that they are simply unable to lose weight anymore, no matter what they do. This was certainly the case for my client Sharon.

Sharon, a woman in her early 50s, came to see me after years and years of relatively unsuccessful therapy. For almost her entire life, she had an extremely difficult relationship with eating and her body image, both of which stemmed from severe sexual and emotional abuse by her father. Food was often used in her family as a way to punish and humiliate her. When I saw Sharon, she weighed over 350 lbs and her medical notes labelled her as morbidly obese. Sharon and I went over what she was eating. On most days, she was actually restricting so much that she barely

ate more than 1000 calories. Of course, this intense restri-
ction would lead to extreme episodes of binge-eating, but
Sharon's high weight was not justified by only these episodes.
Rather, it was the years she spent in extreme restriction and
yo-yo dieting that resulted in her set point increasing so
much that she could no longer lose any weight at all.

The take home message is that when dieting and weight loss is your goal, you are not simply contending with your willpower. You are literally fighting against your body. The consequences may be a lifetime of battles, dissatisfaction, and, paradoxically, increased weight gain in the long run.

To summarise, here are some points for you to consider:

- If you are currently at a healthy weight, ask yourself if it's worth entering a lifetime sentence of restrictive dieting just to get below your already normal weight.

- If you are stuck in the dieting cycle and your body is currently still able to lose weight then consider the long-term effects. Is this how you want to live your life; constantly fighting to maintain this weight? And have you thought about the fact that eventually the dieting may stop working altogether?

- If you are dealing with the consequences of yo-yo dieting, disordered eating, and restrictive-binge cycles, remember to show compassion to yourself. Society often pushes us toward unrealistic ideals without understanding our body's true mechanisms.

No matter your body size or shape, you can prioritise your health, wellbeing, and build a positive relationship with food and eating to create a beautiful life.

> If you're curious about how some people can lose weight and maintain it, the answer often lies in whether they're acting **out of fear or out of love**. Those who start running regularly because they enjoy being in nature, challenging themselves physically, and improving their health, might find weight loss happening naturally. They stay within their set point, perhaps just on the lower end. Their goal isn't to re-strict themselves to shed pounds, but to make positive changes out of self-love and wanting a healthy, strong, and sustainable body.

The challenge lies in discerning who might be stuck in a miserable cycle of disordered eating, as opposed to those who embrace life and treat their body kindly and lovingly. Since we can't truly know what's happening in someone else's life, the best advice is to not get too caught up in comparing yourself to others or judging their body's size and shape. Instead, focus on yourself and what's best for your wellbeing.

If, after reading all of this, you still feel interested in going on a diet, my advice is to go ahead and do it. Dieting is an option–not just for those who haven't started working with me, but even for those who have been in therapy for some time. If you find yourself frustrated with your weight, shape, or size and believe that this is the most crucial aspect of your life, and you're willing to sacrifice everything else for a quick fix that may likely result in ending up even larger than before, then by all means, take that option.

Many people initially respond by saying, "No, I could never go on another diet again now that I understand why it hasn't worked for me so far." However, some might give it one last try, only to quickly realise how it triggers a cycle of food obsession, restriction, small portions, and not eating what they want. Often, this final attempt leads them to a point of readiness to surrender and genuinely consider trying something different.

Fortunately, there *is* an alternative approach to dieting.

"Food is symbolic of
love when words are
inadequate."

- Alan D. Wolfelt

CHAPTER 8:

Making peace with food and eating

Imagine if I told you that every day, you could only go to the bathroom three times, following specific schedules, and had to excrete precisely as instructed during those times. You'd likely think it's preposterous and outright reject the idea. After all, who should have the authority to dictate your bathroom habits? Using the restroom is a natural bodily function that you instinctively know how to handle. It's a knowledge you were born with, and, for most people, it's never been a question. You trust your body to guide you.

Well, if it wasn't made clear enough previously, let me remind you again:

The same is true for eating.

Your body knows how to eat. Trust yourself and your instincts when it comes to food choices.

When people ask me how I assist those looking to transform their relationship with food and their bodies, my answer is simple: "I teach them how to discover what works best for themselves." Whether it's one-on-one coaching, group sessions, or retreats - this concept forms the foundation of all my work. Unless there's a medical complication, most individuals are born with an innate understanding of what, when, and how to eat. They have a natural sense of what their bodies need, and if they truly pay attention to this inner wisdom, it will guide them toward the things that best serve them. This was beautifully illustrated during a training event I ran for a group of eating disorder professionals. I offered the idea that we have an internal *knowingness* of what we want and need to eat. Before I could say much more, a psychologist in the front row put up her hand.

> "My goodness," she said, "I never thought about it like this, but a few years ago I went through a phase where I was really sick. I had terrible diarrhoea, lost weight, got an awful rash, and felt exhausted all the time. At first, no one knew what was wrong with me. My friends and family all tried to give me the best advice they could – eat more nutrients, have a balanced diet, etc. – but all my body wanted was red wine, chocolate, and steak. I thought it was so weird and tried very hard to fight these 'unhealthy' cravings. Just a few weeks later, I finally got results from my doctor. I was diagnosed with celiac disease. It would

seem that my cravings, though seemingly unhealthy, were actually trying to get me away from the foods that were causing my body to really suffer. My body really did know what it wanted."

As we have already shown, our relationship with food is shaped by a complex interplay of biological disposition, personal experiences, beliefs, and learned behaviours. This often leads us to disconnect from our innate wisdom and, consequently, we stop trusting ourselves. The first step therefore is to relearn how to listen to our body's needs. We're now ready to embark on the next step in our journey: Rebuilding your relationship with eating.

BITE SIZED THOUGHT

In my approach, I've drawn inspiration from various food and eating-related methods as well as psychological and ancient techniques. Before sharing my take, I would like to refer you to some fantastic books and resources that have revolutionised how we approach eating and our food experiences. If you're curious about the teaching and models that have influenced my methods, I invite you to explore these texts and their communities: *"Intuitive Eating," "Health at Every Size," "Beyond Chocolate," "The Rules for Normal Eating,"* and others recommended at the end of this book. The main ideas behind all these approaches are that anyone can foster a healthy relationship with food and eating by following their body's signals. If you've spent significant time punishing and distrusting your body's messages, it won't be as simple as flicking a switch to regain that internal signal. Instead, you'll need to go back to basics and relearn (or sometimes learn for the first time) these vital skills.

PART 2

REBUILDING YOUR RELATIONSHIP WITH EATING

"Every time you eat or drink, you are either feeding disease or fighting it."

- Heather Morgan

CHAPTER 9:

The five essential principles

The core idea behind the methods I am about to share is that anyone can cultivate a healthy relationship with food and eating by learning how to connect with their body's signals. By trusting that process, positive changes will unfold naturally. However, it is essential to recognise that if you've spent considerable time punishing and doubting your body's messages, restoring that internal signal won't happen overnight.

Now, let's dive into the five principles that, when followed, will gradually help you rediscover your body's innate ability to make nourishing, enjoyable, and healthy choices when it comes to eating–just as it should be. These principles are:

1. Eat when you are genuinely hungry
2. Trust your innate wisdom to choose the right foods
3. Embrace a mindful mindset
4. Listen to your body to know when you're full and satisfied
5. Have preferences, not rules

BITE SIZED
THOUGHT

In this section, I will introduce some tasks that are labelled as ongoing tasks, because this journey involves self-discovery and relearning. These practical exercises serve as the foundations for revolutionising your relationship with food and eating. They aren't meant to be quick-fix, "in the moment" tasks. Rather, they require dedication over days, weeks, or even months. I encourage you to approach these exercises with curiosity and an open, non-judgmental mindset, ready to embrace the process of learning and growth. Your commitment to these tasks will pave the way for transformative changes in how you perceive and interact with food.

Chapter 10:

Principle One: Eat when you are genuinely hungry

Those with a healthy relationship with food follow their body's cues and eat when they genuinely feel hungry. They don't let clock time, the expectation from others, social standards, or any other external factors dictate their eating patterns. Instead, they listen to their body and respond accordingly. But, if you've been a chronic dieter or have lost touch with your internal appetite, recognising hunger can be quite a challenge. Your body might have learned that signals of hunger are left unanswered until finally it stops sending these signals. On the other hand, you might still experience hunger signals but have ignored them for so long that you're not sure how to interpret them anymore.

Not knowing when you're truly hungry impacts every aspect of your eating experience. If you start eating without genuine hunger, how can you know when to stop? On the flip side, if you resist feeding yourself despite feeling hungry, you might become so ravenous that making wise choices about what or how to eat becomes difficult. At that point, your survival instincts might kick in, encouraging you to devour anything available as quickly as possible, potentially leading to overeating or bingeing.

To transform your food and eating relationship, it's vital to understand and respond to your hunger with love and care. To do so, you need to create a clear scale of what hunger feels like to you. This is a crucial first step in this journey and is an ongoing process with numerous opportunities for growth and learning. The liberating part is that there are no mistakes in this process. Each experience teaches you more about your hunger and helps you discover what truly nourishes your body best.

To begin understanding your hunger, we'll use a scale ranging from 0 to 5. Right now, we'll focus on this aspect solely, but later on we'll merge it with a fullness scale from 5 to 10, creating a comprehensive, continuous scale.

Imagine that the 5 on the scale is neutral, meaning you neither feel hungry nor full. The 0 represents being absolutely starving; you are so hungry, that you feel like you might pass out if you don't eat immediately.

Your goal is to explore the various signals you experience at different points on this scale. What does 4 feel like to you? What about 3, 2, or 1? Pay close attention to physical sensations, such as a growling stomach, salivating mouth, headache, or dizziness; emotional feelings, like mild annoyance, irritability, outright anger, or anxiety; and mental signals, like thoughts about what to eat, where you will go to get food, or even an inability to concentrate. You can investigate these signals separately or observe them together over a period of time. There is really no right or wrong way to do this.

BITE SIZED THOUGHT

If you don't experience any sensations of hunger, I recommend trying a temporary approach to wake up your hunger. For three or four days, consider eating every three hours–this is the only time I suggest a structured schedule for eating. By working with this regimented schedule, you will very likely reawaken your body's innate hunger cues, allowing you to recognise them more effectively. Throughout years of working in this field, I haven't encountered anyone who, after following this approach, didn't come back to me with a delightful surprise–their hunger had suddenly awakened! So, if you were uncertain about your hunger before, you'll likely gain clarity after this period.

Keep in mind that once your hunger returns, you might go through a phase where it feels like you're hungry quite frequently. This is natural, expected, and a crucial part of the healing process. Do not be alarmed about it as it is perfectly normal. This reaction often occurs because your body can't believe it's finally receiving the nourishment it needs. The duration of this phase varies based on how restrictive your eating habits were and how long they persisted. Embrace this journey with patience and understanding as you nourish your body back to a healthier state. It's a positive step toward rebuilding a harmonious relationship with food and your natural hunger cues.

A hunger scale example is shown in the figure below, but don't get caught up with the specifics of this scale. *Your* hunger signals may be different. What you experience at a very low level of hunger might be what someone else experiences at a very high level of hunger.

Hunger scale	Description
5	• My hunger is neutral. I am not thinking about food or eating at all. I can get on with whatever I am doing.
4	• I think I am starting to get hungry but I don't feel like eating anything specific. • I am somewhat craving a snack or something small to eat, but I am not sure just yet what I really want.
3	• I am starting to notice specific cravings or desires for what I want to eat. • I feel like just a snack would not satisfy me. I want real food. • I have lost concentration.
2	• I am starting to feel irritable. • My stomach is making some noises. • I know exactly what I want to eat. I can picture it!
1	• My stomach won't stop grumbling. • I am panicking about where I am going to get food. • I can practically taste the food I am thinking about. • I would eat anything.
0	• I feel dizzy or sick. • I feel like I am going to faint. • I am almost going off food now that I am so hungry. • I cannot focus on anything.

Now that you're familiar with the hunger scale and its nuances, it's time to personalise your experience. Let's put your insights into action by creating your own hunger scale. The exercise below will allow you to develop and finely tune the scale according to your sensations and needs.

LET'S GET WORKING:
Developing Your Personal Hunger Awareness Scale

INSTRUCTIONS: For this exercise, you'll need your journal.

Grab your pen and paper as we walk you through this empowering process. By observing and calibrating your personalised hunger scale over the next weeks, you'll not only heighten your awareness of your body's cues but also foster a deeper connection with your intuitive eating journey.

Instructions:
Set Up Your Scale:
Begin by drawing a line and labelling it from 0 to 5. Allocate some space next to each number for your observations.

Observe and Calibrate:
Over the upcoming two weeks, make it a practice to keenly tune into your hunger cues at various levels. Pay meticulous attention to the physical sensations, emotional shifts, and mental cues accompanying each number on your scale.

Gather Comprehensive Data:

Keep a journal or record of your experiences. Identify when you sense genuine hunger without it becoming overwhelmingly intense. Delve into what distinguishes, a level 4 from a level 2 for you. Consider how the taste and enjoyment of your food change between levels.

Cultivate Curiosity:

Approach this process with a sincere sense of curiosity. Embrace the opportunity to learn about the subtleties of your body's communication. Invite questions such as: How does your body uniquely signal different hunger levels? What emotions or thoughts accompany each level?

Set Reminders:

To maintain consistent engagement in this exploration, consider setting hourly alarms (e.g., every one hour, two hours, etc.). These gentle reminders will prompt you to pause, assess your hunger, and refine your personalised hunger scale throughout the day.

By committing to this exercise, you empower yourself with a profound understanding of your hunger cues. This journey leads to a more harmonious relationship with your body and a greater sense of confidence in navigating your innate wisdom.

Happy exploring!

As you become more in tune with your hunger, you'll also gain clarity on times when you eat for reasons other than genuine hunger. Many factors can lead people to turn to food: boredom, stress, anxiety, jealousy, anger, guilt, and the list goes on. "Emotional eating" is a common term used to describe overeating in response to non-physiological hunger cues. However, the reality is often much more complex than that. In many instances, when we dig deeper, we realise that people are restricting their food intake or denying themselves of the food they really want. Then, when their emotions come into play, their willpower to avoid eating finally gives in, and they end up overeating or bingeing on all their "forbidden foods." So, even though it might seem like emotional eating at first, there are actually many things happening before that contribute to it. Let's look at Jessica's story to make this point clear.

Jessica, a 27-year-old woman, was seeking my guidance about her eating habits. She felt frustrated because she often found herself raiding the pantry late at night. She was convinced that her eating episodes were solely driven by emotional triggers. At first glance, Jessica believed she had a healthy relationship with food because she was not actively dieting and she was incorporating various food groups into her meals. However, as we delved into her life-style and eating patterns, we uncovered a more intricate picture.

Jessica had a demanding job with long hours, which left her feeling stressed and overwhelmed. She dedicated herself to work, often skipping meals during the day to meet deadlines and keep up with her responsibilities. This unintentional food restriction left her body undernourished, but she didn't realise the impact it had on her eating behaviours.

While Jessica's late-night snacking did have an emotional component, such as seeking comfort and relief from stress, it was also her body's response to a prolonged period of undernourishment. The combination of emotional stress and lack of proper nourishment created a cycle where she sought solace in food, especially when exhaustion kicked in.

Through our work together, Jessica started to monitor her hunger cues and prioritise nourishment. As she allowed herself to eat regular, balanced meals throughout the day, she noticed a significant improvement in her late-night snacking tendencies. She discovered that true emotional eating episodes became less frequent when her body was well-fed and cared for.

Jessica's journey highlighted the complexity of emotional eating and its relationship with unintentional food restriction. By addressing both aspects, she began to develop a healthier relationship with food and a deeper understanding of her body's needs. This realisation not only transformed her eating habits but also empowered her to manage stress more effectively and practice self-care consistently.

As you embrace the process of eating when you're truly hungry, you'll discover your own sweet spot–the optimal level at which to enjoy your meals fully. It's like finding that perfect balance where the food tastes its best and satisfies you just right. If you eat before reaching this sweet spot, you might notice that the meal doesn't taste as delightful as it could have when you were genuinely hungry. We've all been there–eating when we're already full and missing out on the full flavour experience.

On the flip side, waiting too long to eat after reaching this level can lead to excessive hunger. At that point, your body just craves anything it can get, and you may find yourself eating mindlessly and too quickly. This overeating happens as a response to the intense hunger you feel.

So, the intention is to find that perfect moment when you're pleasantly hungry–not overly so and not underfed. When you achieve this balance more often, you'll have more enjoyable and nourishing eating experiences. Trust your body's cues and explore your personal hunger scale to guide you on this journey to mindful and satisfying eating. Your taste buds and body will thank you.

CHAPTER 11:

Principle Two: Trust your innate wisdom to choose the right foods

If you haven't developed a secure relationship with food, the notion of giving yourself permission to eat foods that you actually want, without external control or rules, might trigger an overwhelming dread. For many, the concept of being able to eat certain foods without feeling guilt, shame, or disgust, seems impossible. This feeling was vividly illustrated by my client Stacy's experience.

Stacy's journey through adulthood was marked by a cycle of diets and self-deprecation, leaving her feeling terrible about herself. During one of our sessions together, we decided to tackle the challenge of eating a 'forbidden food' item. Stacy chose a slab of chocolate, a treat she hadn't allowed herself to enjoy fully for a long time.

It wasn't that Stacy wasn't eating chocolate regularly; It was more that when she did, it was accompanied by overwhelming negative feelings.

As she hesitantly opened the chocolate bar before me, tears welled up in her eyes.

In that moment, Stacy shared something profound–she couldn't recall a single time in her adult life when she had simply sat with another adult and enjoyed chocolate without guilt or shame. All her experiences eating chocolate were entangled with moments of bingeing or secret indulgence, further perpetuating her distressing relationship with food.

Stacy's emotional response to eating chocolate, highlighted the deep impact that her dieting and restrictive behaviours had on her ability to savour food with genuine enjoyment. When Stacy and I embarked on her healing journey, we focused on breaking this cycle, helping her rediscover a positive connection with food, and finding joy in eating without negative emotions attached. Through self-compassion and gentle guidance, we aimed to create new and healthier associations with 'forbidden foods,' building a healthier foundation for her relationship with both herself and the food she loved.

BITE SIZED THOUGHT

It's common to feel nervous about the idea of "eating what we want." If that thought scares you, it's worth considering that during episodes of bingeing, we consume these so-called "forbidden foods" in much larger quantities than we would if we allowed ourselves to eat them with permission. Moreover, evidence suggests that people who do tune in to their body's cues and eat accordingly, tend to have a lower body mass index (BMI) compared to those who follow restrictive diets. Many individuals who start listening to their bodies are pleasantly surprised to find that what they crave is actually delicious, wholesome foods. It's a common revelation that, when they genuinely listen to their bodies, they have less cravings for snacks or binge foods. Lastly, giving yourself permission to eat what you truly want leads to greater satisfaction and reduces the likelihood of overeating, constant snacking, or experiencing binge episodes.

It's important to understand that what is being suggested here goes beyond mere indulgence. I'm not suggesting that you just start eating all the foods you never allowed yourself to eat before, or that you develop a conditioned intellectual understanding of what's "right" for you. Instead, it calls for tapping into the profound knowingness that resides within you. We all possess this intuitive wisdom, a compass if you may, that guides us towards the foods our body needs and craves. This inner wisdom is not governed by external rules or societal norms but is intricately connected to your unique physical and emotional requirements in each moment. It's this innate knowingness that discerns whether you need the warmth of a hearty pizza, the freshness of a nourishing chicken salad, the lightness of a refreshing bowl of fruit, or the comfort of some thick and delicious ice cream.

Honouring this inner wisdom is a transformative journey towards nurturing yourself on multiple levels. It knows precisely what will both satisfy your taste buds and fulfil your body's nutritional needs. Trusting in this inherent wisdom enables you to break free from restrictive diets and external judgments, cultivating a compassionate and nourishing relationship with food.

Those who have restricted their diet for a long time are fearful that without rules, or external guidance around food, they would solely crave snacks, treats, desserts, breads, pastas, and any of the other foods they've cautiously avoided. There's a belief that they would lose all control and never want to eat a healthy salad again. And of course, the fear of their weight jumping adds to their apprehension. But remember, this is not about succumbing to every craving, nor is it about strictly denying yourself certain foods. Rather, it's about embracing the harmony between **what you genuinely desire and what will best serve your body**. If nurtured correctly, you will soon learn to trust that this innate knowingness will naturally lead you to choose what's best for you.

When first approaching the "Trust your innate wisdom" principle, the challenge lies in identifying and connecting with that internal knowingness and trusting it to aid you in this journey. To start off, it is helpful to be very practical. If you never developed a capacity to feed yourself without external influence, you may feel quite lost about how to choose.

With that in mind, I would like to offer you a checklist–a clear guide to narrow down your options and reconnect with your body's natural appetite when making food decisions. Whether you keep it with you, place it near the fridge, or mentally run through the options, this tool empowers you to decipher what it is that you actually want to eat. Anytime you notice your hunger, you can refer to this helpful guide to help you make a food choice.

Do I want something

☐ Hot	☐ Cold	☐ Sweet
☐ Savoury	☐ Smooth	☐ Lumpy
☐ Crunchy	☐ Light	☐ Easy to eat
☐ Chewy	☐ Filling	☐ Bitter
☐ Watery	☐ Aromatic	☐ Tangy

How do I want to feel at the end of eating?:

☐ Full	☐ Light	☐ Comforted
☐ Heavy	☐ Warm	☐ Refreshed
☐ Energized		

Of course this is not an exhaustive list. It is just a way to help you to connect to the internal guidance of what type of food you may like to eat.

The second strategy involves visualisation and can be used when you find yourself torn between food choices. Often, our ingrained thought patterns attempt to dictate what we "should" eat. For example, you might be browsing the menu in a restaurant and see options like a burger and fries or a healthy chicken salad. Your mind may suggest going for the salad because it's the healthier option, but that decision might not truly align with what your body desires. To break free from these mental constraints and truly understand what your body craves, try this visualisation exercise:

Take a moment to picture each option you're considering. Picture them one at a time. Imagine how it would feel to take a bite of the first option. Pay attention to how it makes you feel, the flavours you experience, and whether you can almost taste it in your mouth before even eating it. Does your mouth start to water in anticipation? Now, repeat this exercise for the other options on the menu. Pay close attention to how your body reacts to each one. Which option seems to resonate the most? Be honest with yourself about what your body is asking for. Is it different from what your mind initially suggested? If so, remember that it's just your old diet-related thoughts trying to influence you. Ultimately, go with your body's intuition and choose the option you genuinely desire. Enjoy your selection to the fullest–savour each bite and take pleasure in the entire dining experience. Remember, it's about listening to your body and finding joy in your food choices!

While this exercise might appear straightforward, it's surprising how frequently we can still find ourselves trapped in our thoughts, talking ourselves out of what our intuition tells us. Trusting the process is crucial in overcoming this.

Let me share some valuable feedback I received from my client, Ray, who learned this lesson during his early experimentation days and vowed not to repeat the same mistake.

"*I visited my favourite restaurant as usual, and checked out the menu. To my disappointment, they had replaced my beloved butternut soup with tomato soup. Now, I'm not typically a fan of tomato soup, but on that day, I had a strong craving for soup, and I could almost taste its deliciousness in my mind. Despite this, I somehow managed to rationalise my way out of it, thinking it wasn't my usual choice.*

I shifted my focus to one of those healthy grain bowls on the menu. One of them contained many ingredients I love, like avocado, quinoa, and currants. Given that these are foods I am fond of, I decided to order the grain bowl. However, when it was served, my heart sank; it wasn't what I truly wanted. All I could think about was the tantalising taste of that tomato soup.

I've learned my lesson. Next time, I'll trust my instincts and choose what my body is genuinely craving!"

Ray's experience demonstrates how important it is to listen to our bodies and not let preconceived notions sway our choices. The more we practise this approach, the better we become at making food decisions that bring us genuine satisfaction.

As you start to change your eating behaviours and choose different foods, keep in mind that this journey is about progress, not perfection! Remember you are learning to think, behave and react in a new way. It isn't easy and not every eating experience will be perfect. What truly matters is that every eating experience is an opportunity for learning.

When things don't go as planned, take it as a chance to learn and reflect on what could be done differently in the future. And when you have successful eating experiences, take a moment to congratulate yourself and acknowledge the significance of the lessons you've learned. These positive moments will serve as valuable motivation during more challenging times. To stay connected with your progress, consider journaling and regularly keeping track of the process and the insights you gain along the way.

BITE SIZED
THOUGHT

As you'll see, we've only just begun to uncover the depth of Principle 2, with a wealth of insights waiting to be uncovered. In the chapters that lie ahead, our aim is to delve even deeper into the intricacies of Principle 2, ensuring you gain a thorough grasp of this foundation before we transition to our exploration of the next principle.

CHAPTER 12:

Conquering
the habit

When you embark on the journey of listening to your internal wisdom, you may find that you have a strong desire towards the foods you've restricted the most. It could be tempting snacks like chocolate, chips, cakes, or popcorn, or perhaps full meals like pizza, pasta, burgers, and bread. Initially, you might feel like these are the only foods your body craves. If this occurs, you might acquire a touch of anxiousness and find yourself wondering about the situation. This is quite normal.

During this phase, it's crucial to grant yourself permission to have these foods. The reason for these cravings is precisely because you *have* made them off-limits for so long. Over time, your body and mind will come to understand that this isn't a binge; these foods are available to you anytime you desire them and they are just as permissible as the "diet foods" you forced yourself to eat. Through this process, the foods which were once forbidden, will gradually lose their power over you.

This transformation is the most incredible part of the healing journey.

Throughout my years of working with clients, I've witnessed countless individuals experience newfound freedom with food–a level of freedom they had never encountered before. At the start, many people approach this concept with scepticism, doubting it could ever work for them. However, in my experience, every single client who continuously applies themselves to this work, eventually gains this freedom. It's a privilege to witness the joy and liberation they experience when the transformation takes place.

Allow me to share one of my favourite examples from my client, Martina. She was initially resistant to the idea, but her journey toward freedom with food turned out to be remarkable.

Martina, a woman in her late 50s, had been struggling with eating disorders and excessive dieting throughout her life. By the time she sought my guidance, she was stuck in a cycle of severe restrictions and regular binge eating. She felt entirely disconnected from her body. Embracing the "trust your innate wisdom" principle seemed daunting for her, so we decided to take it one step at a time. Here are some snippets from our conversations as we delved into this concept:

Romi: *If you had to choose one food that you would not keep in your house because you believe you would binge on it; something that even the thought of makes you nervous– what would it be?*

Martina: *Oh, that would be cheese. Cheese is the big one for me. There is no way I could have it in my house and not eat it all in one go.*

Romi: *OK. So let's agree that you will go out and buy as much cheese as you like. Enough that you could have as much of it as you want anytime you feel like it and not run out. If this feels frightening, remember that when you binge, you eat such foods in much larger quantities than you would eat if you were just savouring it when you felt like it.*

[Two sessions passed. Martina confirmed that she was eating the cheese any time she felt like it. In the third session, she walked into my office and sat down.]

Martina: *There is still cheese in my fridge and I haven't touched it for a couple of days.*

Romi: *What does that tell you?*

Martina: *It tells me that cheese isn't my concern. It's not my main binge food. In fact, I think it's cornflakes. Cornflakes are the problem. I can go through boxes and boxes of it without any control.*

Romi: *OK, let's try cornflakes. Go buy as many boxes of cornflakes that you need to be able to eat it anytime you want cornflakes.*

[A few sessions passed. During this period, Martina ate the cornflakes. Occasionally she did it for reasons other than hunger. However, she largely ate the cornflakes in a loving manner; i.e. at a time when she was genuinely hungry.

She put the flakes in a bowl and ate calmly until she'd had enough.
After this time, Martina came into my office and sat down.]

Martina: *So…there is a box of stale cornflakes in my cupboard. I haven't felt like eating them.*

Romi: *That's interesting. What does that tell you?*

Martina: *(Determined not to believe in the process) It tells me that it's not cornflakes either. It's peanut butter. That is my biggest weakness. It always has been. I can eat jars of it in one sitting.*

Romi: *Are you willing to try peanut butter?*
[During the next five weeks, there were times when Martina ate peanut butter in excess and used it as a coping mechanism, yet it was still less than she would have eaten during her old binges. About a month and a half after we first introduced the peanut butter, Martina walks into my office and sits down.]

Martina: *Well, peanut butter and I have had a falling out. I have two completely unopened jars and I haven't touched the stuff all week.*

Romi: *That's interesting. What does that tell you?*

Martina: *Ok, I get it. I finally understand the process now.*

There are numerous ways to approach exposing yourself to your forbidden foods, and it doesn't have to be as intense or prolonged as Martina's experience. Keep in mind that she had a complex history of eating disorders, and every step we took was carefully discussed and agreed upon. You might simply want to allow yourself to buy a specific food item when you feel like it. For instance, if you crave a cupcake, you can treat yourself to one and enjoy it. When pasta is calling your name, go ahead and make enough for a meal.

Another method to try is a "**food item vacation**." This concept was shared in a workshop by a woman who had been on her journey for some time. She successfully broke free from her struggles with Mars bars by dedicating a weekend to indulge in them intentionally. Rather than bingeing, every time she felt hungry, she'd sit down, open a Mars bar, place it on a plate, and eat it with a knife and fork. The results were truly transformative. She explained that after doing this intervention, she was initially put off at even the sight of Mars bars. As time passed, she noticed that their power over her had diminished. Eventually, she could enjoy the occasional Mars bar without any distress.

As you give yourself permission to eat these previously forbidden foods, you'll realise that they are just like any other food item. Sometimes you'll desire them, and sometimes you won't. In fact, as you truly savour and taste these foods, you might even discover that you don't actually like them as much as you thought. The crucial lesson here is that treating these foods as forbidden only magnifies their hold over you. By allowing yourself to relate to them without restrictions, their power diminishes and you gain a healthier relationship with them.

"The food you eat can be either the safest and most powerful form of medicine or the slowest form of poison."

- Ann Wigmore

Chapter 13:

What about sugar?

It is time to discuss the "sugar villain" narrative that has sparked widespread debate in recent years. Before tackling this, it's important to note that in the past, similar demonization has been directed towards other food groups like fat and carbohydrates. Nutritional trends tend to be ever-changing, with the diet industry eagerly embracing the latest fad only to swiftly move on to the next. The "sugar villain" narrative appears to be the latest addition to this trend.

We can acknowledge there is common consensus that the excessive amount of sugar in our foods and beverages is concerning. Numerous books, documentaries, and studies highlight the negative implications of this and have turned it into a global health challenge that demands change. As consumers, we must educate ourselves, become label-savvy, and take responsibility for what we put into our bodies. Additionally, introducing nutrition education in schools would be highly beneficial to promote informed choices.

However, it's also essential to be aware of the potential negative impacts that may arise from extreme or overly restrictive measures. Some of these negative impacts include a nutritional imbalance resulting from missing essential nutrients found in foods with natural sugars. There are also lower energy levels due to reduced glucose intake; the potential development of disordered eating behaviours; a decreased palatability and enjoyment of meals; social and psychological impact in social settings; a risk of substituting sugar with unhealthy alternatives; and an increased likelihood of binge eating due to intense cravings.

It's fair to say that the discussion offered here cannot encompass the complexity of the sugar debate. Nevertheless, the impact of the "sugar villain" narrative on eating disorders and the general dieting population is significant enough to compel me to at least address it.

It's true that some individuals may experience a perceived addictive quality when it comes to food, especially sugar. Physiological evidence suggests that sugar can activate neural pathways in the brain that are similar to those triggered by other addictive substances. However, it's essential to exercise caution when interpreting such findings. Some claims comparing sugar consumption to cocaine may be exaggerated.

The extent of the association between sugar and addiction is still a subject of ongoing research, and the evidence is often extrapolated from animal studies. Thus, it's crucial to approach these claims with a critical eye. Moreover, evidence indicates that this association may be particularly strong for individuals who are restricting their intake of certain foods, regardless of their episodes of binge eating. In other words, dieting and food restriction can play a significant role in how certain individuals perceive and respond to sugar consumption.

In addition, the connection between sugar consumption and obesity isn't a linear cause-and-effect relationship. For instance, consider individuals from different countries, like the French who are known for their passion for pastries and desserts, or the Swedish, who delight in cinnamon buns or even the Swiss, famed for their delicious chocolates. All three countries showcase relatively high sugar consumption rates. Yet, despite their affinity for sugary delights, citizens in these nations don't face the same obesity crisis seen elsewhere. Their obesity rates are nearly 50% lower than those in the US, as reported by the World Obesity Federation. This observation underscores the multifaceted nature of the obesity issue, influenced by factors beyond just sugar intake, such as cultural dietary patterns, physical activity levels, and overall lifestyle choices.

When working with clients who have a history of substance abuse or addiction, and with those who express concerns about sugar, I approach the "trust your innate knowingness" section with caution, especially in the beginning stages. (This cautious approach also applies to clients with medical conditions like diabetes.) However, I have often observed individuals who claim to have a sugar addiction, but in reality they are caught in a diet mentality. While some may overindulge on sugary foods during binge episodes that lead to physiological impacts, a more significant contributing factor is often the psychological fear associated with certain foods.

The first issue with vilifying sugar is that, when sugary foods are considered forbidden, they become alluring and trigger conditioned responses. This may result in binge eating, creating an illusion of addiction that actually stems from restriction followed by overindulgence.

The second issue with vilifying sugar is that some use "sugar" as an umbrella term to lump together other food groups they want to restrict. If someone tells me they don't wish to eat any processed, manufactured, sugary snacks, that is one thing, but others in the "sugar is evil" camp target sugar in all its forms, including honey, maple syrup, most fruits, and many vegetables. This can even extend to many staples, such as rice, bread, and pasta. These food items are the staple diet for many countries around the world. Ironically, the people in these countries do not suffer from the same obesity and disordered eating rates as are seen in countries who advocate a more restrictive approach.

To find a balanced approach to food, it's essential for individuals to recognise that overly restricting certain foods gives those items unnecessary power. By understanding that these foods are part of a diverse diet and not inherently addictive or irresistibly tempting, individuals can progress towards making choices that promote their overall wellbeing.

BITE SIZED THOUGHT

Principle 2, "Trust your innate wisdom," means learning to trust yourself, which takes time. It's a journey of exploration where you might experiment with eating foods that you once avoided while on diets. During this transformative phase, your weight might stabilise, or you might gain a few pounds. Don't worry. I like to call this stage "the deconstructing phase," where we dismantle all those ingrained beliefs, learned behaviours, and patterns that have shaped us. The goal is to replace them with nurturing, loving, and kind behaviours. This powerful step is essential for breaking free from food obsession and finding true liberation.

"Cooking is like love; it should be entered into with abandon or not at all."

- Julia Child

CHAPTER 14:

The cause and effects of food

So far, we have focused on the first part of the "trust your innate wisdom to choose foods that will satisfy you" principle. The main focus has been to learn to eat what you truly desire, including those foods that were once forbidden. At the moment, your goal is to continue working on this until those foods no longer hold power over you. If you haven't reached this stage yet, that's okay; keep moving forward, and you'll get there in time. However, if you're already experiencing more peace around food, then you can switch your focus to the next part of this principle: finding foods that nourish you. This idea is really about **discovering how different foods make you feel**. It's important to note that these steps are not strictly linear; they inform and influence each other.

Ideally, we'd effortlessly tap into our internal wisdom and choose foods that make us feel great the majority of the time.

However, we can expect to encounter occasional challenges due to old habits and ingrained beliefs. For this reason, we will discuss the techniques that can help with the process. This phase can be quite an organic step along the way, which was certainly the case for my client Paul.

Paul was a recovered binge-eater who had worked hard to trust his own internal wisdom to guide him on what to eat. For example, he honoured his body's cues and desire to eat granola for breakfast–a food that he had long considered off-limits due to its connection to binge triggers. This was a pivotal moment that showcased Paul's newfound trust in his inner guidance. Breaking free from restrictive habits, he could now choose to savour the very food that had once caused turmoil. However, despite this newfound liberation, after doing this for several months, Paul noticed a peculiar pattern occurring. Just two hours after eating his desired breakfast, he would find himself unsatisfied, hungry, and looking to eat again. As Paul continued his journey, he paid close attention to his body's responses to different foods. On weekends, when he had more time, he occasionally craved a breakfast of eggs and bacon. To his surprise, this simple change left him deeply satisfied for hours, with no lingering hunger cravings.

Paul began to realise that while it was essential to embrace the period of eating granola to break free from its negative power, his innate knowingness then guided him to consider not just the foods he craved, but also those that would best serve and nourish his body. The important part was that this understanding didn't come from any diet plan or external explanation. Instead, it emerged from his own personal experiences. Through this process, he began to understand the cause and effect play of his food choices, which empowered him to make more mindful decisions without relying on external guidelines.

As you learn how different foods affect you based on your own experiences, you'll find a greater incentive to make changes out of self-love. When you consistently have negative experiences after eating a particular food, you'll naturally want to avoid it. I recall a friend from my university, who had a fantastic relationship with food. He decided to stop eating pizza because he noticed that consuming too much cheese made his eyelids sweat. That's what I call serious self-awareness!

This process of investigating cause and effect will transition you into loving action. Once you have enough evidence to suggest that a specific food isn't serving you well, you may choose to limit your consumption or eliminate it entirely.

At this point, you will begin making healthy lifestyle choices driven by love, rather than fear. The main focus shifts from emphasising weight, to healing with kindness. Interestingly, many individuals who reach this stage find that even if the healthier option means gaining weight, they still choose what best serves their wellbeing. When weight is no longer the central concern, many people actually start losing weight naturally. It's the paradoxical idea: if you let go of your obsession with weight loss, the weight may just let go of you.

This notion is illustrated perfectly by my client Frank.

Frank, an older man in his late 50s, sought help for his overeating and unhealthy lifestyle, which he believed contributed to his autoimmune disease. Over the course of a few years, Frank and I collaborated on his journey towards positive change. He made significant progress by shifting his focus away from weight-loss as the primary goal and instead concentrated on transforming his relationship with food. Frank abandoned fad diets and learned to listen to his body's true needs. Surprisingly, his weight stabilised for almost two years, which was a complete contrast to his dieting days where his weight was constantly yo-yoing. During our time together Frank conquered his late-night binge habits and successfully employed various tools and strategies that we discussed in our sessions.

One day, Frank called me outside of our occasional check-in sessions. He wanted to share his plan for a juice fast after reading a book and conducting extensive research. He explained that the author of the book also suffered from an autoimmune disease and he was able to cure himself and go off medication through juicing. Based on our work together, he was asking for my opinion and approval. During our call, we talked about the times when Frank had tried restrictive diets to lose weight, but this time was entirely different. Frank was motivated solely by his health. He even expressed that his wellbeing mattered more than any potential weight loss, and if the program didn't serve him well, he'd discontinue it, even if he lost weight.

Frank embarked on a 30-day juice fast. He didn't weigh himself during this time, he felt satisfied, and he didn't experience any instances of bingeing. Most astonishingly, his autoimmune-related skin condition seemed to clear up. In the end, Frank shared a heartfelt note, recognising that his ability to undertake this journey was only possible because he had first addressed his issues related to food and eating. Frank's transformative experience highlights the power of a mindset shift from weight-focused diets to a genuine focus on health. By developing a positive relationship with food, he unlocked the door to a successful and empowering juice fast that prioritised his wellbeing over mere weight loss. And yet, once his fast was over and he did finally weigh himself he had lost a whopping 30lbs- yet he described the experience as being "as dull as looking at the time on my watch."

"Tell me what you eat,
and I will tell you what
you are."

- Jean Anthelme Brillat-Savarin

CHAPTER 15:

Becoming label-savvy

Many years ago, while strolling through a supermarket, I witnessed an inspiring moment: a young boy of about eight years old asked his mother to buy a particular cereal. In a wise response, the mother offered a challenge. "If you are able to read all the ingredients on the label and tell me what they are, then we can buy it." As the boy tried to decipher the complex names, he eventually stumbled upon "Trisodium Phosphate." Quietly, I noticed he simply put the box back.

Understanding what we eat is crucial. It goes beyond memorising nutritional values and calorie contents from past dieting days; it's about reclaiming full responsibility for what we put into our bodies. Just like we may refuse to eat a plate of dirt, we shouldn't mindlessly consume items without knowing what they are. Some added ingredients can be far worse than eating dirt!

As we shift from mindless to mindful eating, it's important to cultivate an understanding of the sources that nourish us. This, of course, opens the door to more extensive discussions, including ethical, moral, environmental, and sustainable considerations. While these topics go beyond the scope of this book, they are essential aspects of conscious eating and taking responsibility for our wellbeing.

BITE SIZED THOUGHT

If reading labels triggers diet-like behaviours for you, it's okay to take a step back from it for now. When you feel ready to delve into this aspect, you can revisit it later. Striking the right balance is crucial–supporting your progress without promoting avoidance or denial of your food choices. Ultimately, awareness of what we consume is a fundamental stepping stone for shaping our approach to food.

When exploring labels for this purpose, you want to shift your focus to the ingredients, rather than fixating on calorie, fat, or sugar content. How deep you delve into this is entirely up to you. You might decide to avoid anything that sounds like it came from a chemistry lab, opting for natural ingredients. On the other hand, you could choose to eat something regardless of its contents, even if it's as unlikely as dirt, sand, or hair–yuck!

The purpose of this exercise is not to tell you what you should or shouldn't be eating, rather it is to cultivate the habit of knowing what you're eating. Empowering you to make conscious choices about what you put into your body.

"Transformation is not
five minutes from now; it's
a present activity. In this
moment, you can make a
different choice, and it's these
small choices and successes
that build up over time to help
cultivate a healthy self-image
and self-esteem."

- Jillian Michaels

CHAPTER 16:

Principle Three: Embrace a mindful mindset

Just on its own accord, even without any of the other principles, when it comes to food and eating "embracing a mindful mindset" can truly be a life-changing experience. With mindful eating, the world of food opens up in ways you have never imagined before. Here, you embark on a journey of tasting, savouring, and appreciating the flavours and textures that surround you. It's an adventure of curiosity, where you can distinguish how food feels the moment it touches your tongue compared to the sensations it brings after some time.

There are diverse definitions of mindfulness that can stem from ancient traditions all the way to modern psychological lexicon. For the purpose of our exploration, we will specifically focus on the definition of mindfulness accepted among psychology experts:

The practice of being fully present and aware in the moment without judgement.

Mindful eating, in particular, involves bringing this heightened awareness and non-judgmental attention to the act of eating. It means engaging all your senses to savour and appreciate each bite, acknowledging the flavours, textures, and even the love and effort that went into preparing the food. Mealtimes become more than just the meal; they become a daily practice. Over time, this will extend to other aspects of your life. By honing your awareness during meals, you start cultivating mindfulness in other moments throughout your day.

The best way to grasp the power of mindful eating is by experiencing it firsthand. In every client session, group workshop, or retreat, I prioritise opportunities to practise and explore mindful eating together. Most of this section will provide you with experiential and practical tasks to work on when you eat. You should aim to follow the prompts and reflect on the experience. The more you invest in these practices, the greater the rewards it will bestow upon your life and you'll witness how mindful eating has the potential to transform your relationship with food and enrich your entire existence.

LET'S GET WORKING:
Experience Mindful Eating.

INSTRUCTIONS: For this exercise, you'll need your journal.

⏳ *10-15 minutes*

In this practice, we will explore the art of mindful eating through a series of sensory experiences. To prepare for this exercise, you will need some small food items. Here are some options that would be good for this task.

FOOD OPTIONS
Apple slice
Grapes
Piece of chocolate
Potato chip
Any type of nut
Small piece of a celery stick
Cracker
Clementine segment
Raisin

Choose two or three items from this list (or something similar that you have at home.) It is good to work with different tastes and textures during the experience. You can then do the same exercise again and again using different foods.

If you scan this QR code with your phone, you will have the option of hearing this exercise with audible instruction instead of reading it.

Once you have the food ready–follow the prompts below to complete the tasks. Spend about 2-3 minutes on each prompt.

Look at your food

Hold the item of food in your hand. Start by just looking at it. Really look at it. Notice what thoughts come up about this food. What are the sensations you experience by simply looking at it? They may be good, they may be bad. Don't judge, just observe them.

Smell your food

Bring the food to your nose and gently inhale. What do you smell? Is it as you expected? Is it pleasant? Notice the compulsion you may have to quickly put this food in your mouth as you normally would. Just sit with that feeling.

Feel your food

Bring the food to your lips. How does it feel? Slowly place it in your mouth but don't bite down or eat it yet. Feel it in your mouth. Notice yourself starting to salivate. Observe how hard it is to stop yourself biting down right away. Feel the flavours that start to seep into your mouth.

Taste your food

Bite down. What are the flavours? Chew slowly. What are the textures? Notice the compulsion to rush the chewing. Observe how the tastes change the more you chew. Try to chew without swallowing for as long as you can. Once you swallow, slowly observe as the food runs down your throat.

"Those who think they have no time for healthy eating will sooner or later have to find time for illness."

- Edward Stanley

CHAPTER 17:

Mindful eating techniques

In this chapter, we will explore a range of techniques designed to cultivate mindful eating. These practices aim to foster a deeper connection between your mind and your meals, helping you savour each bite, make conscious choices, and develop a more gratifying relationship with food.

Mindful Plating

Many of my clients have shared stories of moments when they overindulge: the secretive pantry raids, munching straight from the bag, or a late-night fridge rendezvous with a chair as their companion. While I believe there are no rigid rules about "what to eat," I wholeheartedly advocate that we can manage "*how* to eat."

One powerful technique that can transform your relationship with food is the practice of "Mindful Plating." By taking the time to put your food on a plate and sitting down to eat it with a knife and fork, you elevate your eating experience from a mindless and perhaps guilt-ridden action to a conscious and responsible act. Mindful Plating is not about stopping certain behaviours. It's about doing these behaviours with a level of conscious awareness and with choice. Even if you are engaging in a full-blown binge episode, you can still opt to do so in a mindful way–with full acceptance, knowledge, and no judgment.

Furthermore, the act of putting your food on a plate compels you to make a conscious decision about the quantity you're eating. Gone are the days of being dictated by the size of the packet or serving size that encourages you to mindlessly finish off the last few bites. When you portion your food onto a plate or in a bowl, you empower yourself to be more mindful about your consumption. And should you desire a second helping, by all means help yourself. This moment becomes an opportunity to pause, check in with yourself, and ask if you genuinely want more, or if you are just eating out of habit.

ONGOING TASK

LET'S GET WORKING:
The Mindful Plate Challenge

INSTRUCTIONS: For this exercise, you'll need your journal.

This straightforward yet transformative exercise invites you to embark on a journey of mindful eating. For at least one day, make a dedicated commitment to place every morsel of food you consume onto a plate. Whenever you feel the urge to eat, take a moment to find a comfortable spot to sit down and present your meals and snacks on a plate. Regardless of how small the item may be, this can be done even if it's just a single chip!

As you engage in this challenge, take some time to reflect on your experience and consider the following points:

• Did you notice moments when you unconsciously reached for food?
• Did you find yourself consuming food without being fully aware of it?
• Did you observe any judgement if you forgot to plate your food?

By becoming more aware of these automatic eating habits while remaining committed to the practice of mindful plating, you can begin to cultivate a more conscious and connected experience with your food relationship

Silent Serenity

In today's bustling world, we often find ourselves mindlessly munching away amidst an array of distractions. Whether it's the TV on in the background, our phones demanding constant attention, or the chatter of colleagues, we rarely take a moment to truly appreciate our food. When we fail to pay attention to what we're eating, we miss out on enjoying the eating experience. This lack of enjoyment can leave us feeling unsatisfied and disconnected from our body's cues, making it challenging to know when we've had enough.

Interestingly, this also works in reverse. The distractions themselves can drive us to eat impulsively. Think about it–do you find yourself reaching for a snack every time you watch a particular TV show? Do you mindlessly munch on popcorn at the movies? These habits stem from linking eating to external triggers instead of genuine hunger or pleasure.

And so enters "silent serenity." This transformative technique is a personal favourite of mine. By eating in silence without distraction, you are able to embrace the eating experience with undivided attention, immerse in the flavours, and feel a newfound sense of fulfilment and nourishment.

BITE SIZED THOUGHT

There is still a very social component to eating that I think is important and wonderful to embrace. On the whole, I love having meal times with family and friends. During these moments we talk, laugh and enjoy ourselves while eating. Nonetheless, I am strict about other forms of distraction while eating. We have no TV, music, phones, or other distractions at the table. Occasionally, as a family, we agree to enjoy our meals by eating in silence. I understand this may not suit everyone, but it's worth considering or trying on occasion. Many clients express initial concerns about eating in silence, fearing discomfort or awkwardness. However, unless there's a specific trauma associated with silent mealtimes, most people discover that silence enhances their eating experience and brings remarkable benefits. In fact, occasionally my 8-year-old son will spontaneously ask, 'Can we just have a quiet breakfast today?' It warms my heart to see how simple moments of silence can be so meaningful and enjoyable for everyone.

LET'S GET WORKING:
Eating Free From Distractions or Noise

INSTRUCTIONS: For this exercise, you'll need your journal.

⧗ *15-35 minutes*

This task is about eating free from distractions or noise. Choose one meal where you think you will be able to do this. Sit quietly, and slowly and mindfully eat your meal. Don't talk to others and keep other distractions away or off, such as TVs, music, the radio, reading, and phones.

If the idea seems daunting, start gradually. Begin by taking a few initial bites in complete silence, and then extend the time as you feel comfortable.

Reflect on the process:
• Was this an enjoyable experience or did you find it challenging?

Take note of the thoughts that crossed your mind during the process.

Notice how this experience changed your eating habits:
• Did you eat more or less?
• How did the food taste?
• How did you eat compared with how you normally eat with distractions?

Timeful Eating

Many years ago, a diet gimmick introduced a plate that would switch between red and green lights–a rigid system where green meant you could eat, and red signalled you to stop until it turned green again. Sadly, this approach was driven by control and weight loss, fostering a lack of self-trust and confidence, rather than a healthy relationship with food. However, a similar concept with a different intention actually brings forth a beautiful approach to mindful eating.

We've all had moments when we have rushed through a meal, barely realising what we've devoured–sandwich, chips, and a banana gone in a blur, devoid of true enjoyment. But perhaps you've also experienced the sheer delight of eating when fully immersed in the moment, free from distractions and noise. Now, it's time to embrace the power of time itself in our eating habits.

Welcome to "Timeful Eating." As you learn to be fully present during your meals, you'll notice how the act of allowing yourself ample time to eat can transform your dining experience. No more rushing through meals–instead, you'll savour each bite, appreciate the flavours, and truly enjoy the nourishment.

Many people find this next exercise to be challenging. It may not be suitable for regular practice, unless, of course, you genuinely enjoy it. Its purpose is simply to emphasise the contrasting experience of eating when you have ample time and to notice the compulsive habitual tendencies or even discomforts that arise when consuming food at a slower pace.

LET'S GET WORKING:
The 30 Minute Challenge

INSTRUCTIONS: For this exercise, you'll need your journal.

⏳ *35-40 minutes*

In this exercise, you'll have the opportunity to explore the art of truly savouring a meal. Select one meal in your day where you can dedicate a full 30 minutes solely to eating. The key objective is to explore the art of mindful eating and to genuinely take your time with your meal. The intention is not to eat continuously for the entire duration or to increase your food intake. Instead, focus on savouring your meal slowly and thoughtfully.

You might find this exercise very uncomfortable. If you do, just remind yourself it is just a one-off exercise.

As you undertake this challenge, keep in mind the following instructions:

- Try to extend the act of eating over the entire 30-minute period or for as long as you comfortably can.
- Avoid rushing through your meal; take deliberate and mindful bites.
- Pay close attention to the taste, texture, and aroma of your food.

During and after the challenge, reflect on the following questions:

- How did the experience of eating for 30 minutes compare to your usual eating pace?
- What was it like to eat so slowly and mindfully? Were there any particular challenges you faced?
- What thoughts came to mind while you were savouring each bite?
- Did you notice any differences in how the food tasted compared to your usual eating speed?

Remember, the aim is to make this a mindful and eye-opening experience, without any pressure to eat more or differently than usual.

Sacred Dining

Imagine if every time you sat down to eat, you created a special ceremony to mark the occasion. You set the right mood, ambiance, and intention to enjoy your meal with conscious awareness. Not only does this enhance your dining experience, but making it a habitual practice can also help curb unwanted, mindless eating behaviours.

In religious settings, meals often begin with a blessing, intending to infuse the act of eating with significance and gratitude. This is a beautiful practice for many and certainly carries positive intentions. If this is something that resonates with you, it is certainly encouraged. However, some people hold negative associations with religious rituals. Therefore, there are alternative ways to create a beautiful ceremony around your meals, fostering a mindful and enjoyable eating experience. Consider these delightful options:

- Light a small candle, symbolising the illumination of your senses.
- Place fresh flowers nearby, embracing the beauty and vibrancy of your meal.
- Say a few kind words, setting a positive tone for the delightful feast ahead.
- Hum a line from a favourite tune, infusing your meal with a touch of joy.
- Close your eyes, and take a serene 20-second pause to connect fully with the present moment.
- Share a conscious smile with yourself, radiating gratitude and contentment.

====== *ONGOING TASK* ======

LET'S GET WORKING:
Creating Mealtime Rituals

Choose a ritual that suits your preferences. You have the option to incorporate this ritual before significant meals or any time you go to eat. Try experimenting with both approaches to discover what resonates with you. Choose a ritual that is simple to remember and has the potential to become a lasting habit in your daily routine.

Bountiful Appreciation

Have you ever paused to truly appreciate everything that goes into you having food? Let's take something as simple as a banana and delve into the journey it takes to reach you. The sun's warmth and timely rain nurture the banana plant, while dedicated workers tend to the crop, hand-picking the fruit at its peak ripeness. It might have travelled from distant lands, involving countless individuals–lorry drivers, collection and transportation teams, and warehouse workers–who played vital roles in delivering it to your local store.

Then comes the effort you invested in acquiring that banana. You took the time to go to the store and exchanged your hard-earned money for this nourishing delight. Reflect on all the work that went into the money you earned, and the people who supported you along the way.

Even for something as seemingly simple as a banana, a beautiful symphony of time, effort, work, and love comes together to bring it to your table. This is what "Bountiful Appreciation" is all about: Embracing a profound sense of gratitude for every morsel you eat and recognising the countless hands and hearts that contributed to this nourishing journey.

ONGOING TASK

LET'S GET WORKING:
Gratitude in Every Bite

Before every meal today, allocate just one minute to reflect upon the intricate journey your food undertook to reach your plate. Consider the effort of those who grew, harvested, prepared, and transported it. Express a sincere thank you for this nourishment, and then proceed to savour each bite with mindful attention. As you do, notice how this heightened awareness enhances your perception of the flavours, textures, and overall eating experience.

Chapter 18:

Principle Four: Listen to your body to know when you're full and satisfied

Discovering the art of recognising fullness follows a remarkably similar path to that of understanding hunger. We will now extend the hunger scale and add levels 5 to 10, where 5 represents a neutral state (neither hungry nor full), and 10 represents feeling absolutely full or even "stuffed," as if you might become sick from overeating.

Once again, the exciting part is decoding your own unique signals for the various points on this scale. What sensations differentiate a 6 from an 8? How do you recognise when you've reached a 7? And ultimately, what level of fullness do you find most comfortable for yourself? It's important to remember that everyone's preferences differ in this regard, and that's okay! Some individuals relish the feeling of being quite full after a meal and then wait several hours until hunger arises again. Meanwhile, others prefer not to feel overly full and opt to stop eating earlier, but also eat more frequently. In essence, there's no definitive right or wrong when it comes to your fullness scale–it's all about what your body feels most at ease with. To develop your personal fullness scale, it's crucial to stay tuned in to your body while eating. Every few mouthfuls, take a moment to check in with yourself and ask, "How full do I feel right now?" Observe your food for cues as well. For instance, the first few bites may taste quite different from the last few. At what point does this shift occur for you? An inspiring example of this comes from my client, Josh, when he created his own fullness scale.

Josh, a 27-year-old man, was exploring his fullness scale with me. He had spent the two weeks prior to our session checking in with himself regularly while eating. He stated that he notices when he gets full because his mind starts to get distracted from the eating process. "When I suddenly get the urge to look at my phone, even if it's not on the table with me, that's when I know I am no longer eating due to hunger."

Below is an example of a completed fullness scale. Remember this is just one example. Your fullness signals may be different, or, you might experience things at a different level compared with this example:

Fullness scale	Description
5	• I am not thinking about food or eating at all. I can fully focus on whatever I am doing.
6	• The food is delicious and delightful. I am completely engaged in my meal and happy while eating
7	• I start to feel a noticeable sensation in my stomach as it begins to fill up. • I am getting slightly distracted and less interested in eating. • I have negative thoughts like, "I'm eating like a pig."
8	• I know I am just eating for the sake of it. My thoughts are telling me enough is enough but I just keep going. • I am feeling heavy in my stomach.
9	• I am so full I feel like I could burst if I keep eating. • Strong pulling sensation in my stomach. • I am producing saliva in my mouth.
10	• My stomach is actually in pain from overeating. • I feel nauseous or have already vomited. • I have eaten so much, I can barely move.

LET'S GET WORKING:
Your Personal Fullness Scale.

INSTRUCTIONS: For this exercise, you'll need your journal.

Now it's your turn to develop your own personal fullness scale. You will need a notepad or a piece of paper with a scale from 5 - 10 and space next to each number to write your learnings. Over the next two weeks, immerse yourself in creating and refining your very own fullness scale.

The more dedication and attention you devote to this, the more attuned you'll become to the subtle nuances of your body and mind when it comes to feeling satisfied. Remember, we're not just talking about physical signals here; we're delving into the realm of emotions and thoughts as well, creating a holistic understanding of your unique fullness experience.

Just as you did with your hunger scale, you want to approach this process with a sense of curiosity and a genuine desire to learn about yourself. It's a fascinating adventure of self-discovery, where you'll uncover valuable insights.

It should be noted that this principle, "Listen to your body to know when you're full and satisfied" is truly the natural and delightful result of a harmonious relationship with the other principles, rather than a standalone concept in its own right.

Picture this: you begin your meal when you're at that ideal level of hunger. You naturally choose dishes you love that provide nourishment and enjoyment. You eat mindfully, fully aware of each bite, taking your time to taste what you are eating and then your body effortlessly guides you to stop when you're satisfied. It's like a graceful dance of intuition and self-awareness that guides you towards a contented and fulfilling end to your meal.

"To eat is a necessity, but to eat intelligently is an art."

- La Rochefoucauld

CHAPTER 19:

Establishing your body's preferred eating range

Now that you have grasped the intricacies of hunger and fullness individually, it's time to combine the scale to create a continuous one that will guide you to discover your body's personal preferred eating range.

What you will discover is that you may prefer eating before reaching a hunger level 3 or 4, and stop at a satisfied level of 6. Or perhaps you will find that you enjoy experiencing deeper hunger and may delay eating until you reach a 2 but then stop at a 7 or 8 which results in longer breaks between meals. You should also remember that your preferred range is not static. It might change based on factors like climate, time of year, and daily activities. Stay flexible with the scale as an evolving guide rather than a strict rule.

Here's my personal example of how the scale works in practice:

> *My body tends to prefer fewer meals with longer intervals.*
> *When I do eat, I enjoy wholesome and satisfying meals.*
> *Yet, every few weeks or so, I notice my body craves more*
> *regular eating for a couple of days. During those times, I*
> *opt for lighter options like fruits or toast in the morning,*
> *followed by a mid-morning snack. I find myself less hungry*
> *for a whole lunch but prefer smaller, more snacky foods.*

It's essential to note that this is my pattern, developed from years of paying attention to my body. Your pattern may be completely different. In fact, if you are underweight or not eating enough, you may find your body's natural pattern right now guides you to simply eat more. Just let your body guide you. Sometimes this may mean eating less, but for many that can also mean eating more. Take the time to discover how your body likes to eat and honour it, even when it changes.

As you embark on your journey of exploring fullness, you might encounter various eating "traps" that arise from learned behaviours. Although we have already delved into our habitual eating patterns, it's essential to revisit them as we pay closer attention to our eating behaviours. The more at ease you become with your eating experience the more you can confidently tackle these traps head-on.

Here is a list of common habit traps that you may encounter, along with guidance on how to address and transform them.

Habit trap	Alternative behavior
Finishing all the food just because it's on the plate.	Purposely leave a little bit of food on your plate every time you eat so you get used to being comfortable with leaving food.
Eating according to the bag size of a particular snack (chips, chocolate, sweets, etc.)	Use a 'decanter' technique. Take all your snacks out of their packets. For instance, if you have a big slab of chocolate, open it up and break it into pieces. Then, anytime you want some, take what you desire from the jar. This way, you are guided by your appetite, not by marketing or packaging suggestions.
Over-eating in order not to be rude to others	Have some practised phrases ready that are kind but assertive, allowing you to politely decline overeating. For example, say, "That looks delicious, but I am really full, and eating more would make me uncomfortable. I'll pass this time," or "If it's alright with you, I'll take the remaining portion home, as the meal was delightful, but I'm quite full right now."
Always ending a meal with something sweet.	Challenge yourself for a few days to skip ending your meals with something sweet to see if it's a habit or a genuine craving. If you still feel satisfied without it, you'll know it was just a habit that can be changed.
Letting thoughts tell you that you *think* you have had enough–regardless of how physically hungry or full you are.	Take a moment to tune into your body. Consult your fullness scale to gather valuable data. Let your body, not your thoughts, guide your eating decisions.
Stopping when you have reached the maximum number of calories for the day, irrespective of whether you are full.	Shift away from strict dieting and treat yourself with kindness and compassion. Listen to your body's hunger and fullness cues instead of rigid calorie limits.

"Eating is not merely a material pleasure. Eating well gives a spectacular joy to life and contributes immensely to goodwill and happy companionship. It is of great importance to the morale."

- Elsa Schiaparelli

CHAPTER 20:

Principle Five: Embrace preferences, not rules

In many ways, "embrace preferences, not rules" is the most important principle to remember. Without it, this approach could easily turn into just another rule-based diet, albeit a less harmful one compared to many others. This principle reminds us that none of the previous four principles are rigid rules, and none are meant to be followed strictly. Instead, we can think of them as guiding preferences that help build a balanced and sustainable relationship with food.

Let's face it: sometimes you'll find yourself indulging in a delicious piece of pie when you're not even hungry, and that's okay. There will be moments when that lasagna is too good to resist, and you might eat a little past fullness–and that's fine too. When life gets busy, mindful eating might not always be possible. You might be juggling responsibilities, chasing after kids, or swamped with work, leading you to grab a sandwich on the go and eat it while multitasking. There will even be occasions when you just can't have the exact food you desire, but making do with what's available is perfectly acceptable. Our main goal here is to focus on your preferences rather than restricting you with hard and fast rules. A great illustration of this principle comes from my client, Jade.

After a year of dedicatedly tuning in to her body, Jade had gotten very good at listening to her body's cues. She learned to respect her hunger, which meant there were occasions when she accompanied her family to meals without being hungry herself. It took some confidence, but she managed to decline food when she felt full, even if it meant disappointing others who offered her dessert. Jade had also become adept at getting the food she truly desired. For instance, on a day when her family opted for Mexican cuisine but all she craved was pizza, she confidently went ahead and got her pizza fix. Similarly, when her friends insisted on a Chinese restaurant outing, but she was in the mood for a light salad, she fearlessly ordered just that, sticking to her preferences.

However, during one of our sessions, Jade recounted a recent experience where she was out with her family, and they all decided they wanted to get fish and chips. While Jade desired something lighter, she couldn't help but notice the discomfort that arose from not having precisely what she wanted. In that moment, she recalled hearing my voice in her head, emphasising the importance of not becoming too rigid with the principles we'd explored together. It struck Jade that she had been quite strict with herself, and though it had been necessary at the beginning of her journey, she realised that even this approach had started to resemble diet-like behaviour.

A liberating thought crossed her mind: "It's only food. I don't have to eat the exact thing I want every single time." With that newfound realisation, she chose to enjoy the fish and chips, recognising that while it wasn't her initial desire, it turned out to be incredibly delicious!

"Success is the sum of small efforts repeated day in and day out."

- Robert Collier

CHAPTER 21:

The interconnected nature of the principles

It's essential to recognise that all the principles are interconnected–not a linear progression nor independent of each other. Although they might initially appear separate, they work together harmoniously to create a loving and nurturing approach to eating. Often, people encounter challenges in this journey because they inadvertently overlook one of the principles. Clients will share that they are still struggling with binge eating during our sessions, and upon closer examination, we often discover that one specific principle has been neglected.

The culprit could be not honouring their hunger, restricting themselves of desired foods, mindless overeating, or failing to listen to their fullness signals. When this happens, it's crucial to remember that many of us have spent years following fear-based, unconscious eating patterns, and breaking free won't happen overnight. It takes time. Remember that progress is what we seek, not perfection. Celebrating even the smallest moments of freedom becomes significant–savour the experience of the first time you were hungry to the right amount. Or a moment when you ate exactly what you wanted. Be aware of the time you tasted each mouthful with mindful awareness and celebrate that you stopped eating when you were completely satisfied. It is in these **pearl moments** that your eating wisdom will grow and you will be certain that even through the difficult moments, this is your path to freedom.

To end this part, I will share a beautiful example shared to me by a client, Alice, from the first time she experienced the freedom of love-based eating.

> *"A close friend of mine was unwell and ended up in the hospital. Now, I must confess, hospitals aren't exactly my favourite places, but I knew I had to be there for her, no matter what.*
>
> *After spending a good hour by her side, I finally said my goodbyes and left her room. As I stepped out, I couldn't ignore the hunger pangs that had started gnawing at me. Waiting until I got home didn't seem like an option, so I made my way down to the hospital lobby where they had a Starbucks.*
>
> *Typically, I'd force myself to go for the light and healthy option like a salad, but this time, it was different. I felt drained and cold, and what I really craved was something comforting and filling. So, brace yourself, I finally did*

what we've been working on—something totally out of character that I have actually never done before—I ordered a cheese and roasted vegetable panini!

With my panini in hand, I found a cosy table in the corner of the room and sat with my back to everyone, not because I was ashamed, just because I really wanted to focus on what I was eating. I took my first bite and it was as if a wave of flavour washed over me, and I was immediately captivated by how incredible it tasted. It was perfect. I swear at that moment it felt like the most delicious thing I had ever eaten. I took another bite, slowly, with intention. I wanted to taste every crumb. I didn't need to think about how to eat it mindfully; that was exactly what I wanted to do, naturally. Just eat with total awareness. Each bite was like a hug from the inside. It filled me up with the nourishment I needed. Not once did I think about the fat content, nor calories, nor 'being bad.' It felt like the most loving thing I could have ever done for myself at that moment. I never had an eating experience quite like this…"

"Your true nature is untouched by praise or blame, success or failure. Recognize your intrinsic worth beyond the judgments of self and others."

- Dhammapada

PART 3

BODY IMAGE & EXERCISE

"Your body is a temple, but only if you treat it as one."

- Astrid Alauda

CHAPTER 22:

From self-judgement to self-acceptance

It is impossible to talk about food, eating, diets, and disorder, without bringing exercise and body image into the equation. In fact, for some individuals, the challenges related to exercise and body image are central to the disorder itself. Although there is a significant overlap with what you've already learned and discovered, it's essential to address body image and exercise as distinct aspects.

In this part of the book, we will explore the harsh self-judgments individuals often make about their weight, shape, and size, gaining insight into how these judgments drive disordered eating behaviours. We'll tackle the relentless struggle with distorted body image, offering strategies to conquer these inner demons. The importance of stepping off the weight loss treadmill and leaving behind the scale will become apparent, as you discover the benefits of focusing on more meaningful health goals. We'll also discuss how clothing choices and shopping can impact your body image and guide you toward a more compassionate approach. Finally, you'll learn to shift your perspective from punitive exercise to joyful movement, making physical activity a positive aspect of your journey towards recovery. Throughout this section, you'll find valuable insights and practical strategies to cultivate a healthier relationship with your body and yourself.

CHAPTER 23:

Your judgements about weight, shape, and size

To delve into this subject, let's start with a reflection exercise, similar to ones you've done before. Take this opportunity to explore your own intricate and deeply ingrained beliefs and biases concerning your body, weight, shape, and overall size.

LET'S GET WORKING:
What are your judgments about weight, shape, and size?

INSTRUCTIONS: For this exercise you will need your journal.

⏳ *15-20 minutes*

This exercise invites you to think about the thoughts and feelings you have about size, weight, and shape in general, not those directly relevant to you.

Contemplate about the following:
What do you think and feel when you see someone who is overweight?

What are your judgments about the attractiveness of someone who is in a large body and why?

What are your judgments about the success level, intelligence, honesty, and morality of people in larger bodies?

What about someone in a smaller body? What do you think or how do you feel about them, their attractiveness, and their characteristics?

Can you identify where these thoughts and feelings come from? Where did you hear these narratives? Did they come from any prior causes, cultural beliefs, environmental factors, social constructs, family narratives, or lived experiences?

Take some time to reflect on what you may have uncovered in the exercise above. These are the prejudices and habitual thinking patterns that exist. But, where do they come from?

We often form generalised views about people based on certain labels, such as "fat," without truly understanding the context. These judgments typically arise when we lack personal experiences that relate to their struggles. To illustrate this point, I would like to introduce you to the following three case examples: Meredith, Holly, and Richard.

Meredith:

At 51 years old, Meredith's body is labelled as "clinically obese." Despite her difficulty in walking, she cares for her little dog and takes him for short walks daily. During one of our sessions, she shared a hurtful incident from earlier that day. Two slim ladies ran past her while she was out with her dog. One of them turned to the other and said through a cruel laugh "You see, that's why we run, so we don't end up like her…"
What these ladies don't know is that Meredith has endured severe physical, sexual, and emotional abuse throughout her life. She struggles with eating, often going days on just 300 calories before succumbing to a 10,000+ calorie binge. Her eating difficulties stem from a long battle with anorexia and bulimia, and she has attempted suicide four times. Her life is a constant struggle against these inner demons.

Holly:

Holly, a 30-year-old executive, seems to have it all–success, beauty, and a slim figure. From the outside, everything appears perfect, and Holly plays along with this facade. However, there's a hidden truth that nobody, not even her husband, knows about. Holly secretly struggles with bulimia, vomiting her food five or six times a day. Despite her achievements, she battles low moods and feelings of exhaustion. She despises her body and is tormented by societal beauty standards. She yearns for others to take her seriously beyond her appearance, and her assessment session revealed the stark contrast between how she perceives herself and how others perceive her.

Richard:

Richard is a 46-year-old man, who has gone through a significant transformation. He used to be teased for being "chubby," but in the last two years, he lost an immense amount of weight, and has become incredibly slim. Many people who haven't seen him in a while admire his newfound appearance and inquire about his weight loss journey. However, what they don't know is the true reason behind his transformation. Richard's weight loss is a result of a severe stomach illness that led him to undergo two major surgeries and multiple procedures. The pain he experiences on a daily basis is excruciating and has forced him to close down his business. Despite his improved external

*appearance, his health, confidence, and even his marriage
have suffered greatly during this challenging time.*

Understanding the context behind why someone is a particular
way can significantly alter our automatic judgments. When we
grasp the context, it often sparks a surge of compassion for the
other person as we begin to comprehend their experiences and
struggles. The initial generalised beliefs we held about them
tend to dissolve once we learn about their story.

Let's put this idea to the test: Look back at the reflections you
wrote for the exercise above and imagine if each judgement
came with a detailed backstory, similar to the case examples
mentioned earlier. Do you feel different about your judgments
now? If the answer is yes, then it might be worth considering
this approach the next time you catch yourself making judgments about others. Simply ask yourself, "**I wonder what that
person's story is and what life factors (both positive and
negative) have shaped them into the person they are today?**"

Remember, the goal is to humanise the people whom you
judge, allowing you to recognise that each individual carries
their own unique set of experiences that have influenced the
way they exist in their bodies. By embracing this perspective,
we foster understanding and empathy towards others, embracing the complexity of human lives.

BITE SIZED THOUGHT

A good example of this was illustrated in the 2019 movie "The Joker." The movie exposes the complex network of social, psychological, economical, and environmental factors that contributed to the development of the so-called "evil character." Instinctively, when we hear about a serial killer who dresses up like a clown and terrorises an entire city, we would automatically have judgments and opinions about that person. But many people watching the movie reported that they found themselves sympathetic to the character as they could see the multitude of factors that came into play, which contributed to him ultimately partaking in such cruel behaviours. Knowing the context helped them to see things from a different perspective.

Sometimes, people find themselves making judgments not just about individuals but entire groups. However, even in these cases, it's possible to explore the "collective story" behind these perceptions. For instance, let's say you have judgments about an entire population living in certain areas of the United States. Perhaps you believe that the majority of people in that state are overweight, neglect their health, and rely on fast food, sodas, and beers. It's effortless to lump everyone together and voice such judgments, and there may even be some truth to the observable behaviour. However, it's crucial to consider the multitude of factors contributing to these patterns on a larger scale. What if these people were never taught how to nourish their bodies properly? What if economic constraints force them to resort to cheap and convenient fast food because they lack knowledge or struggle to afford healthier options? Perhaps their lives are filled with hardships, and a visit to a fast-food restaurant is the only thing that brings them a moment of joy or happiness amidst their challenges.

Moreover, in some cultural groups, body ideals differ significantly from what you might consider "positive." For instance, preferences for body types may vary in African and Latin-American countries compared to those in France or the US.

By opening yourself to the possibility that there's more to the situation than what meets the eye from your perspective, you can cultivate greater compassion and understanding for others. It's essential to recognise that people's behaviours and appearances are shaped by a complex interplay of factors, and considering these broader contexts can lead to a more empathetic outlook.

Why is this all so important? Well, if you're catching on, you may be realising that the automatic judgments we make about others stem solely from our own beliefs and perspectives. These judgments have nothing to do with the other person, as evidenced by the fact that our opinions often shift when we gain insight into their context or situation. Therefore, delving into how you perceive other people is, in essence, a journey of self-discovery. That is, you learn about yourself by seeing how you view others. This realisation held particular significance for my client Katie.

Katie and I had recently begun our work together, exploring the automatic body image judgments she held. During a session, she recounted an incident from the past week. While walking in her apartment complex, she noticed a girl she had seen before but never spoken to nor knew anything about. This girl had what Katie described as a model's body. However, as the girl passed by, Katie found herself flooded with judgmental thoughts.

"She must have such an unhealthy relationship with food." "I bet she has to completely control her eating to look like that." "She must not be a very nice person."

As we delved deeper into the origins of these judgments, I asked Katie, "Since you don't know anything about this girl, how can you be sure if these judgments are true or not? Where did they come from?"

After a thoughtful pause, Katie replied, "They come from me. All of these judgments are reflections of my own insecurities. I struggle with an unhealthy relationship with food, trying to control my eating to achieve thinness, and I often feel like I'm not a very nice person because I'm so caught up in judging others."

This moment of realisation was powerful for Katie as she recognised that her judgments about others were intrinsically linked to her own self-perceptions and struggles. It became evident that exploring how we perceive and judge others is an opportunity to uncover deeper aspects of ourselves.

The general beliefs we hold can serve as a mirror to understand how our minds perceive and project onto ourselves, others, and the world at large. While some of these beliefs may already be known to us, and we might be highly conscious of them, there could also be unconscious and surprising aspects that reveal themselves when we examine them more closely.

Try this for yourself: Recall a time when you had negative thoughts about someone you barely knew or had never even spoken to, whether it is a neighbour, an acquaintance, or even a celebrity. Reflect on the judgments you had at that moment, like, "That pretty girl must be such a bitch," or "That guy looks like a knucklehead," or "Those kids are so spoiled" and so on. Now, think about how different your perception of them became when you actually met and had a genuine conversation with them. Or, if it was a celebrity, perhaps you saw them in an interview or read an article that portrayed them in a completely different light. Those initial thoughts or judgments were formed before you knew anything about them, so they must have come solely from your mind and had nothing to do with the people themselves.

This also works the other way around. Think of a time when you had positive thoughts or impressions of someone, and, as you got to know them better, you began to see them differently. The initial sweetness and goodness you saw in them also originated from your own loving and kind beliefs.

Sometimes, when I discuss this with clients, the response is that even after getting to know others, some people find it challenging to let go of certain judgments. They may feel sympathy for what the person went through, but negative thoughts persist, such as, "How could they let themselves get like that?" or "She has put on so much weight," or "Why doesn't she just eat something? She looks like a skeleton." If this happens to you, don't be too hard on yourself. There's no need to feel guilty or judge yourself for experiencing these thoughts. These ingrained beliefs and thought patterns are very powerful and are a product of our past conditioning, learned behaviours, and unconscious reinforcements. Recognizing this complexity is the first step to freeing ourselves from limiting beliefs. By challenging, and ultimately changing, these beliefs, we can develop new, compassionate, and kind thought patterns that empower us to see others and ourselves in a more understanding light

If all of this seems a bit confusing, let's try an analogy to clarify the concept: Imagine a young puppy brought to an owner, who shows no care and neglects to train it properly. The puppy spends many hours alone and ends up peeing on the couch, forming a habit. Since no one teaches the puppy that this behaviour is wrong, it continues without correction.

Now, imagine that the puppy is taken to a new home and the new owners are not given any indication of the puppy's previous ownership. The puppy immediately pees on the couch. Should the puppy be blamed or punished for not knowing any better? The new owner's initial instinct might be "yes," but had they known the puppy's backstory of neglect and lack of training, they would have understood that it couldn't know any better.

Now, let's take it further. Imagine the owner not only neglecting the puppy but also reinforcing and encouraging the couch-peeing behaviour. In such a scenario, if the puppy goes to a different home and repeats the same action, can it be blamed at all? Or is it simply acting out what it was taught?

Now, let's connect this to ourselves. Imagine replacing the puppy with you. Replace peeing on the couch with all the negative judgments you have about body image, and replace the negligent owner with a society, culture, family, or friendship group that reinforces destructive, unrealistic, and unkind views about body appearances–what's considered desirable, acceptable, or even labelled as gross.

Just like the neglected puppy, the judgments and beliefs we carry about body image may have been shaped by the environment we grew up in and the influences around us. When we understand this, we can begin to see that these judgments might not be a true reflection of who we are but rather learned behaviours and beliefs. This realisation allows us to challenge and change these harmful beliefs and develop a more compassionate and understanding perspective towards ourselves and others.

I hope you're beginning to see that, much like the puppy, your thoughts regarding body image have been trained or conditioned within you. Consequently, you didn't really have a choice but to perceive it that way...**until now**.

As we become aware of these automatic thoughts, we gain the power to reflect on them, challenge them, and truly understand their nature as nothing more than conditioned patterns of thinking. Once we reach this point, we can make a conscious choice whether to continue clinging to these thoughts as absolute truths or see them for what they are – beliefs shaped by conditioning that we can choose to accept or release.

BITE SIZED THOUGHT

At the initial stages of recognising these automatic judgments, people often report feeling upset and overwhelmed. Some even express sentiments like, "My mind is a shit show," or "Seeing all this chaos and negativity is exhausting," or "I must be such an awful person." However, it's crucial to remember that these judgments existed whether we were consciously aware of them or not. By being truly honest, open, and aware of them, we can gain deep insights into our habits, beliefs, and automatic thoughts. This newfound awareness empowers us to identify what we actually want to change.

Chapter 24:

Your body image demon

Now that we've looked at body image related thoughts in general, it's time to explore your own body image story, and, particularly, where some of your ideas about body image have come from.

LET'S GET WORKING:
Uncovering Your Body Story and its Origins

INSTRUCTIONS: For this exercise, you'll need your journal.

⏳ *10-15 minutes*

This exercise is designed to help you unravel your body story and its origins.

Identify Negative Judgments:
- What negative judgments do you currently hold about your body? Write down these judgments in your journal. Be honest and open with yourself.

Highlight Messages from Various Sources:
- What messages have you received throughout your life regarding how your body should look?
- What messages have been conveyed by the media, peers, family, or society?

Examine Contributing Factors:
- What life events, behaviours, habits, thoughts, and situations have influenced your current body? Did you experience instances such as excessive dieting, traumatic experiences, physical health issues, medical conditions, bullying, and more?
- How have these factors impacted your relationship with your body?

As you engage in this exercise, approach it with self-compassion and a desire for understanding. By un-
covering the layers of your body story and tracing its
origins, you empower yourself to reshape your relationship with your body in a healthier and more positive
way.

As you gain awareness of how your mind was conditioned to
perceive body image, you may come to appreciate that you
were never given the chance to see yourself differently. The
body-shaming you heard during your childhood, whether
about yourself or someone else, has lingered with you, influencing every diet, binge, and weight-related hardship. The unkindness, self-criticism, and deprecating language you internalised
over the years were simply a product of the way you were taught
to judge things as good or bad. However, this judgement is not
grounded in reality; a body is simply a body. Whether we view
it as good or bad is influenced by a multitude of factors and
conditions.

By acknowledging the various causes and conditions that
shaped your current body, you may be able to cultivate a deeper
understanding and compassion towards yourself. You'll realise
that the suffering, shame, guilt, and blame you subjected yourself to were unjustified. Furthermore, in recognising that the
negative judgments you have about others often stem from
your own self-judgement, you can probably surmise that deve-

loping more understanding and compassion for yourself will lead to a positive shift in how you judge others.

A breakthrough in this aspect was observed with my client, Gill.

Gill had been working hard on developing a compassionate outlook on her thinking and behavioural patterns. As a result, she was showing greater kindness towards herself and her body. However, she still found herself struggling with automatic judgments when she saw her own reflection or encountered people with larger bodies.

Then, during one of our sessions, Gill shared a powerful encounter involving her neighbour's son, who had always been a larger boy. She recalled that his weight often fluctuated, and, on this occasion, he looked larger than she had seen him in a while. As he approached her, she couldn't help but see his discomfort as he awkwardly tried to adjust his tight T-shirt and hide a visible roll over his jeans. Each step he took seemed burdened by an invisible weight that no scale could measure.

In the past, such a situation would have triggered judgement in Gill. But this time, something clicked inside her. Instead of judging him, she felt an overwhelming sense of empathy and compassion. She realised that he, like herself, had his own struggles and challenges. It was as if she could see beyond his appearance and connect with the person he truly was.

This experience had a profound impact on Gill. From that point on, she stopped judging others based on their appe-

arance. She learned to embrace empathy and understanding, appreciating that everyone has their own story and battles to fight.

As you delve deeper into your self-awareness and explore the negative beliefs, thoughts, feelings, and behaviours about your body, you might be wondering how you can shift them into more loving and accepting ones. Luckily, evidence shows that when you focus on one aspect, the other aspects will naturally follow suit. It's like a domino effect—altering your thoughts can influence your behaviours and vice versa. So, by working on these different aspects individually, you can bring about significant changes relatively quickly. However, you do need to actively engage in these techniques to witness a difference.

In the following chapters, we'll dive into a comprehensive set of detailed techniques that aim to help you transform your relationship with your body. From changing your thoughts to modifying your behaviours, each technique plays a vital role in fostering a more positive and accepting connection with yourself.

"Your body hears
everything your mind says"

- Unknown

CHAPTER 25:

Dare to say it out loud

In many cases, people tend to be lenient or even sympathetic towards their negative self-talk. Some people believe that being tough on themselves will make them strive for improvement, thinking it's justified and fair. However, the reality is that if being mean to ourselves truly had a positive impact on our bodies, we'd probably see results by now. Perhaps this strategy isn't as effective as we think. What's even more intriguing is that people often speak to themselves in a way that they would *never* dare to speak to someone else.

In my workshops, I use an eye-opening exercise to illustrate this phenomenon. Participants are asked to reflect on something related to their bodies that they find disgusting or uncomfortable. It could be a particular body part, a number on the scale, or simply how they feel in their own skin. Then, I instruct them to write down exactly how they talk to themselves, even if it includes harsh profanities. For example, if you were looking at your bottom in the mirror and have the thought, "Look at my big, f——ing disgusting fat ass," you should write down this exact phrase.

Next comes the revealing part. Participants are told to pair up and share their written thoughts with each other, using the exact words they wrote down. But the exercise doesn't end there. They are asked to say those words to the other person, as though they were speaking about them: "*You* have a big, f–ing disgusting, fat ass."

The reactions are remarkable. Some faces turn white with discomfort. Others laugh nervously, as they realise how absurd and uncalled-for their self-talk sounds when spoken aloud. There are those who outright refuse to utter such hurtful words to another person. Many experience a surge of compassion when they learn that people with bodies different from their own also struggle with similar thoughts. By the end, the tears are flowing. The exercise becomes a powerful mirror, reflecting how we would never dare say such things to other people, yet we readily subject ourselves to this harsh treatment. It's a poignant realisation that leaves a lasting impact on almost everyone in the room.

Now it's your turn.

LET'S GET WORKING:
Experience the Impact of Your Words

INSTRUCTIONS: For this exercise, you'll need your journal.

⏳ *10-15 minutes*

This exercise allows you to explore the impact of your self-talk on your body image.

There are two ways to do this exercise:

Option 1: Individual Approach
- Take some time alone to reflect.
- Identify the specific negative words or phrases you typically use when thinking about certain aspects of your body.
- Write down these negative words or phrases exactly as you would say them to yourself.
- Now, imagine you are speaking these words to someone else or simply saying them out loud to yourself, paying attention to how they sound.

Option 2: Partner Approach (Recommended)
- Find someone you trust and feel comfortable with to join you in this exercise.
- Let your partner know that they will play a role in this exercise by listening and supporting you without judgement.

- Share the negative words or phrases you usually say to yourself about your body with your partner. Be honest and open.
- Let your partner repeat these negative words and phrases. listen to them as if they were speaking about themselves.
- Afterwards, discuss your feelings and thoughts with your partner, sharing the impact this self-talk has on you.

Remember, whether you do this exercise alone or with a partner, it's essential to go through each step to gain insight into the influence of your words on your body image.

Be kind to yourself throughout the process.

Realising that the way we talk to ourselves is something we wouldn't want to share out loud, let alone with another person, can be incredibly empowering. However, it's crucial to keep in mind that the issue isn't solely about the words themselves or their meanings. The key focus is on setting a boundary and **refusing to tolerate any further negative self-talk**. The commitment to stop accepting such harmful inner dialogue, is known as making a **"zero-tolerance commitment."**

BITE SIZED THOUGHT

The "zero-tolerance commitment" is a potent concept found in various therapeutic models. At its core lies the resolute decision to draw a line in the sand and take harmful behaviours "off the table." This commitment isn't about suppressing thoughts; it's about setting boundaries and refusing to act upon or engage obsessively in detrimental ideas that stand in the way of one's growth and development. What's truly remarkable is the sheer power of this commitment. For instance, in the context of Dialectical Behavioural Therapy, some therapists refrain from providing psychological support to individuals actively attempting self-harm or engaging in high-risk behaviours. Understanding this consequence often becomes the force driving clients to wholeheartedly embrace the commitment and that alone is the catalyst for them refraining from self-harm. Armed with the strength derived from this empowering commitment, clients are then able to address the other challenges they face without the interference of damaging and harmful life threatening behaviours.

When I first introduce this concept to clients, I often receive the response, "There's no way I could stop responding to my thoughts." But the truth is, you're actually doing it all the time. Consider this: When someone angers you, you (hopefully) don't react with acts of violence. That's self-control. Or, when a reckless driver cuts you off on the road, even if you momentarily entertain the idea of retaliation, you don't actually smash into their car. You have the capability to resist those impulsive thoughts. Likewise, when you encounter an incredibly attractive stranger on the street, you don't just force a kiss. These everyday examples demonstrate that you possess the power to refrain from acting on every passing thought that comes to mind. It's just that you've arbitrarily chosen to respond to certain thoughts you deem acceptable, such as the unkind ones about your body.

The key lies in adjusting your acceptability standards. By doing so, you'll find that you can let those uncomfortable thoughts pass without acting on them, ultimately gaining control over potentially harmful behaviours. It's a matter of recognising your innate capacity for self-control and redirecting it towards fostering positive changes in your life.

CHAPTER 26:

Replace or repair antidotes

Even if you've made a "zero-tolerance commitment" and you are working on refraining from self-deprecating speech, there may be times when you automatically slip back into unkind thoughts, negative speech, or unwanted behaviours. The good news is that we have two supportive strategies to use when this commitment is challenged: the "replace" and "repair" antidotes.

The "**replace**" **antidote** involves swapping your harsh self-talk with a more caring, kind, and accepting inner dialogue. For instance, if you catch yourself thinking, "Look at my disgusting fat ass," you should stop and replace it with something like: "My worth isn't solely based on how my body looks; I am more than just my appearance." At first, you may not fully believe these kinder words, but keep at it. It's okay to "fake it till you make it." Just as the years of negative self-talk made those beliefs sink in, consistently telling yourself the kinder messages will eventually make you believe in your inherent worth.

However, there may be moments when even the "replace" antidote doesn't immediately work. That's when you can turn to the **"repair" antidote.** If you catch yourself engaging in harsh self-talk for a prolonged period–say, 10 minutes, an hour, or even a whole day–it's time to counteract it with a deliberate act of kindness towards yourself. What form this act of kindness takes is personal and unique to you. And remember, what feels genuinely kind and helpful to one person might not resonate the same way with someone else. So, find what makes you feel nurtured, supported, and cared for, and embrace that as your repair antidote.

Here are some of the repair activities that people use as helpful acts of kindness:

- Go for a walk
- Take a warm bath
- Give yourself a delicious nourishing meal (meaning exactly what your body wants, when it wants it)
- Get a massage
- Do something creative like singing, painting, drawing, etc.
- Go to bed at a decent hour
- Dance
- Speak with someone you care about
- Watch a nice movie

The essence of this technique lies in ensuring that whenever we catch ourselves thinking negatively about ourselves, we swiftly revert back to kindness. It's like training our minds to understand that, regardless of our thoughts or actions, we always deserve kindness, compassion, and love. The exciting part is that the more time we dedicate to showing ourselves respect and kindness, the faster we will witness significant progress. Consistency in self-compassion fuels our journey of self-improvement and personal growth.

It is important to remember that these simple kindness techniques are only aids. They are not the end goal in and of itself. You don't want to get in the habit of allowing yourself a flurry of negative speech and then simply putting a self-care bandage on it when you're done. Whilst this may be an improvement on simply being unkind and never repairing the action, it won't result in long lasting change. Ideally, you want to be catching these thoughts as they materialise and remember your zero-tolerance commitment, cutting them at the source. Picture it like nipping negativity in the bud. The repair method should only be used as a fallback when nothing else has worked.

ONGOING TASK

LET'S GET WORKING:
Applying the Replace and Repair Antidotes

INSTRUCTIONS: For this exercise, you'll need your journal.

This exercise should be used on a regular basis until the practices of replace and repair become automatic. In the beginning, it is useful to do both replace and repair each time you find yourself breaking your 'zero-tolerance' commitment.

- Write down the negative thoughts or statements that you continue to make about yourself.
- Replace it with a more loving, kind or realistic statement
- Identify a kind action you can take towards yourself to counteract the negative self-talk.
- Repeat this exercise for the other negative thoughts or statements you can recall.

These examples show you how you may apply the techniques:

Negative Self-Talk	Replace Antidote	Repair Action
"I hate my stomach, it's flabby and gross."	"My stomach may not be perfect, but it's a part of me and it's okay to have imperfections."	Take a relaxing bath.
"I can't wear that outfit, my thighs are too big."	"My thighs are just a part of my body, and they're not good or bad, they just are."	Go for a walk in nature.
"I'll never be beautiful or attractive."	"Beauty comes in all shapes and sizes, and I have many positive qualities beyond my appearance."	Write down three things you appreciate about yourself.

BITE SIZED THOUGHT

The reason many interventions don't work is because they focus solely on repair behaviours as the ultimate solution. While these practices are valuable, they often don't provide the complete toolkit needed to genuinely challenge and transform lifelong patterns. In fact, from where we stand, they're merely scratching the surface of the journey towards meaningful change.

"Health is not about the weight you lose, but about the life you gain."

- Dr. Josh Axe

Chapter 27:

Take a weight loss break

One of the most crucial steps for changing your relation-ship with your body is **taking a break from trying to lose weight**. It is a key part of the process and one that often evokes fear and confusion for many people, even by merely thinking about it. Before we delve into why this break is essential, let's clear up any misconceptions surrounding the weight loss break:

- It's not an invitation to indulge in reckless eating habits.
- It doesn't entail actively pursuing weight gain.
- It doesn't mean neglecting exercise or your overall physical health.

A weight loss break means you put losing weight on the backburner. Your every action and decision is no longer about the weight, shape, or size of your body. Picture it as a purpo-seful shift in focus, stepping away from the constant preoccu-pation that you are used to.

Instead, you use this as a time to pause and explore healing, reconnecting with food, eating, and caring for your body, all independent of its appearance. You can imagine it as a treatment phase, where you prioritise your wellbeing, just as someone would while battling an illness. Many individuals, while dealing with various health issues like fertility challenges, thyroid problems, or undergoing cancer treatment, experience body changes. During such times, they often shift focus towards prioritising getting better rather than fixating on body dissatisfaction. It's the same here, you purposely let concerns about your body or shape take a backseat as you concentrate on making peace with your image.

This is best exemplified through my client, Larry.

Larry, a man in his late 40s, struggled with body dissatisfaction and carrying extra weight for years. As part of our sessions, I introduced Larry to food and eating protocols and proposed the idea of taking a weight loss break. However, Larry was sceptical, and our conversation went like this:

Larry: *If I stop monitoring my weight and trying to lose it actively, won't I just keep gaining more and more weight?*

Romi: *Let's explore this together. When did you first start actively trying to lose weight?*

Larry: *About 20 years ago.*

Romi: *And in those 20 years, how many times did you let go of trying to lose weight completely?*

Larry: *Maybe a few weeks here and there, but the desire to change my weight was always there. I don't think I ever truly let it go.*

Romi: *Over those years, has your weight remained constant?*

Larry: *No, it's gone up steadily.*

Romi: *So, when you've tried to monitor and control your weight, you still ended up gaining in the long run.*

Larry: *I suppose that's true. But maybe it's because I lack willpower.*

Romi: *From our conversations, it's clear you've taken extreme measures for a long time to try and maintain a certain body image and avoid weight gain. That doesn't sound like someone lacking willpower.*

Larry: *I guess you're right. I probably say that out of frustration. I just can't figure it out.*

Romi: *Well, consider this: the very outcome you fear by not constantly monitoring yourself is happening despite your efforts. So, what if we try a different approach? Let's break away from what hasn't worked and see if this new perspective leads to a different result.*

Larry: *When you put it like that, I don't have much to lose.*

Larry's journey illustrates how stepping away from the relentless pursuit of weight loss and adopting a weight loss break can lead to a fresh perspective and potentially yield more positive outcomes. Although he didn't lose weight right away, his weight stabilised, and for the first time in years, he was able to maintain it with ease. This shift in focus from constant monitoring and striving to lose weight, to a loving approach that was not focused around weight loss not only improved Larry's relationship with food but also contributed to his overall well-being.

Chapter 28:

Ditch the scale

Taking a weight loss break also means giving yourself a much-needed break from the scale. This may be a total game-changer for transforming your relationship with your body.

Think about it: each time you step on that scale, you're either celebrating or feeling disheartened. This constant reminder that your weight (i.e. your body) is not where you want it to be–or it is but you have to work super hard to maintain it–becomes a huge obstacle to building a healthier body image. When you're embarking on your path to a healthier relationship with your body, it's important to bid adieu to the scale.

The experience of using the scale changes completely after doing this work. You could use the number on the scale to observe and challenge any lingering beliefs that still exist with the intention to gain even more freedom. Or, you could go on it to reinforce how little effect it has on you. When you can stand on the scale and genuinely not be impacted by the number, you know you are free from the scale. Weighing your-self or not, simply won't matter anymore.

This was illustrated by Sheneen, an astute 23-year-old woman who came to see me.

Sheneen sought my help for body dissatisfaction and binge eating behaviours that had troubled her for two years. After our first session, she committed to taking a weight-loss break and decided to stop using the scale, which she had been checking about three times a day.

Over the course of 10 sessions, Sheneen made remar-kable progress in a surprisingly short time. As we neared the end of our work together, we agreed that in our final session, she would step on the scale again. On that day, before weighing herself, we discussed her journey. Sheneen expressed, "I feel so free now. I eat without guilt, I'm in control, and I don't obsess over my body constantly. I even enjoyed a girls' weekend without a single worry about how I looked in a swimsuit. No matter what the scale shows, this freedom is worth it..."

When I asked her to predict her weight, she guessed the number would be less than her weight when we started working together. As she stood on the scale, it revealed that she had not lost anything at all. Surprisingly, Sheneen responded with a smile, saying, "I honestly don't care."

Sheneen's incredible transformation showcased that her self-worth and happiness were no longer tied to a number on the scale. She had found freedom and self-acceptance beyond any numerical measure.

Chapter 29:

Dressing for self-worth

The daily reminders of how we perceive our bodies go beyond just the scale. Our choice of clothing plays a significant role, too. Take a moment to think about what is inside your closet. Do you have pants from five years ago, kept with the hope of fitting into them again? Or do you still have that one dress worn after an extreme diet that you received compliments on? How often do you try them on, fixating on the weight you need to lose to wear them again?

And it doesn't end there. We regularly force ourselves into clothing that no longer fits, ignoring discomfort and signs that we may need a larger size. Why? Because we fear admitting defeat or giving in to the reality of our changing bodies. We put up with waistbands digging into our stomachs and bra straps leaving clear marks on our skin. We even ignore the gaps between stretched buttons on our shirts because we'd rather stay in the same size than dress our bodies in what they truly need.

Holding on to ill-fitting clothes is about more than just physical discomfort. It's a poignant act that speaks volumes each time we choose not to dress according to our current shape or size. In those moments, we unknowingly send ourselves a hurtful message, whispering, "I am not worthy of clothes that fit properly," or "My body, as it is, doesn't deserve acceptance." These subconscious whispers chip away at our self-worth, leaving us feeling shamed, undeserving of love, and lacking any confidence.

To break free from these harmful patterns, it is essential to clear out your closet. Let go of anything that no longer fits without holding back. It's a powerful move to release yourself from the past and embrace change. If you want a drastic change in your life, you need to make drastic changes.

LET'S GET WORKING:
Before and After Closet Clean-Out

INSTRUCTIONS: For this exercise, you'll need your journal (and a strong will).

⏳ *As long as it takes!*

This is a two-part exercise that will to help you shed the clothes that no longer serve you

Part 1: The Before
Prior to cleaning out your closet, write down some of your biggest worries, concerns, or feelings about doing this. Don't hold back or think there's a right or wrong answer. This is just about seeing the reasons why you don't want to change.

The Actual Clean Out:
(Suggested rules)

- Give yourself plenty of time to do this. If you rush it, you will make allowances or dissociate from the experience.
- If it hasn't fit you for over a year, get rid of it.
- Don't just pile and store the clothes in a garage or something. Even knowing that they are somewhere in your reach will result in thinking that at some point you will come back to wearing these clothes.
- Don't hold back on items you deem to be sacred. The suit you wore at your wedding, the shirt from the

first time you held your newborn baby–whatever it is, if it doesn't fit you, let it go. Clinging to it will not magically change your body, so accept where you are at right now and let it go.

Part 2: After the Clean Out.

Now, write down your experience of actually doing the clean out. In particular, focus on these questions:

- Was it hard?
- Did it feel liberating?
- Did the experience differ from how you thought it would be?
- Did you have a hard time with some items?

Remember, there are no right or wrong answers here. In fact, whatever your experience, you will gain some very important insights. It is really important to be honest about how this experience felt.

People often come up with various excuses to keep clothes that no longer fit or avoid buying new clothes that do fit. I've heard a range of reasons from financial limitations like "I can't afford new clothes" to sentimental attachments, such as holding onto a dress worn on a first date or a football shirt that sparks memories of fun times. This sentimentality is completely understandable and valid. The intention here isn't to advocate for discarding every item you own. Many pieces in your wardrobe are undoubtedly beautiful and may hold cherished memories. After all, you wouldn't have bought them if you didn't feel a connection. However, it's crucial to recognise the underlying relationship you have with these clothes and what they symbolise–often, a yearning for a thinner past version of yourself. By keeping certain clothes primarily as a connection to a previous you, you might inadvertently be resisting full acceptance of your present body.

Remember, you don't need to purge *everything* you haven't worn in the past year. Some items are practical, like sports attire, while others are necessary for specific occasions, such as trips to colder or warmer climates. The key is to mindfully consider the reasons behind holding onto clothes that no longer align with your current body or lifestyle, rather than rigidly embracing an all-or-nothing approach.

Chapter 30:

Going shopping

Once you've cleared out your old clothes, you might find yourself needing to head to the store to buy new, well-fitting ones. However, if you're grappling with body image issues, this seemingly simple task can become emotionally challenging and exhausting.

Through years of supporting clients in this process, I've noticed that the experience is deeply influenced by the mindset one brings to it. Those who approach it with a strong intent to break free from the cycle of suffering, obsession, and unkindness towards their bodies, respond differently compared to those who still believe that their weight, shape, and size hold the key to lasting happiness. This striking contrast was evident in two clients I worked with, Olga and Barbara, who both struggled with body image issues.

Olga, a woman in her early 40s, grappled with intense body dissatisfaction and self-loathing. Wearing clothes that were too small for her added to her daily distress. As we discussed the idea of letting go of old clothes, Olga presented numerous excuses, particularly insisting that it would be too expensive to replace them, despite the fact she had a stable job and decent income.

During our time together, Olga rarely attempted the experiential homework tasks I offered between sessions. When we broached the topic of her buying clothes that actually fit her, she was deeply reluctant, expressing that shopping caused her considerable distress, and she was certain it would make her feel worse.

I reflected on her preconceived notions, explaining that her expectations were likely to influence the outcome. As expected, in our next and final session, Olga reported that her shopping trip had been a disaster. She tried on a couple of items, loathed her reflection, and left the store empty-handed.

It became evident that Olga wasn't fully committed to changing her current situation, despite her discontent. When I gently confronted her about this, she became emotional, recognising the truth in my words. She acknowledged her resistance to accepting her situation and making efforts to bring about change.

Following that session, Olga decided to discontinue our work together. While she despised her current situation, she wasn't ready to take the necessary steps towards self-acceptance and transformation.

BITE SIZED THOUGHT

Not everyone is ready to embark on the journey of transformation. Occasionally, I meet with clients who are hesitant to let go of dieting and are seeking an instant fix or a magic wand to make it all better. Just like Olga, some may be reluctant to commit to the hard work required for transformation. If you find yourself relating to this, it's still valuable to explore and reflect on the ideas presented here. I've also encountered numerous clients who weren't initially prepared when they first sought my help. However, in time, some returned with newfound readiness and determination, and remarkable progress ensued. Even if you're not ready to take action right away, consider keeping these insights in mind. You may discover that the right moment for meaningful change will eventually arrive.

In contrast to Olga, here is the story of Barbara, a 60 year-old woman who had been struggling with her body image and constant yo-yo dieting for most of her life.

Barbara was fed up with diets and struggled with self-hatred. We worked on her food and eating behaviours, and she began to experience a newfound sense of freedom and liberation. Despite these positive changes, her body image still caused distress. We explored the concept of acceptance rather than love, and although even that felt challenging for Barbara, she agreed to give it a try.

With Christmas approaching, Barbara was facing a family event where she had nothing fitting or making her feel good. Despite the fact that she did not enjoy shopping, she agreed to give it a go. When our next session came around, Barbara was gleaming. She told me that she had gone shopping with no expectations. She was simply open to whatever would come up. She said that she went into a store and saw a beautiful pants and top set in her current size. Delightfully, Barbara reported that not only did it fit her like a dream, but both in the shop and at the event itself, strangers she had never met came up and commented on how beautiful the outfit was and how lovely she looked. Barabara was flooded with joy as she recalled this. She said she couldn't believe that even at the size she currently was, she could find clothes that felt comfortable, looked great, and even won her compliments. The experience didn't necessarily lead Barbara to love her body, but it undeniably helped her develop a more positive and accepting relationship with it.

CHAPTER 31:

Body acceptance

One message I often share with clients is, "**You don't have to love your body, but you do have to accept it as it is.**" This leads us to a vital aspect of transforming your relationship with your body: Acceptance.

While numerous body positive movements do incredible work by breaking down stigmas, addressing fattism, and challenging unrealistic social "norms," it's important to acknowledge that not everyone may find that deep love for their body, and that's perfectly okay. Attributing self-worth solely to the physical form, whether positively or negatively, can have its challenges. Even if you feel good about your body, any threat to that belief might trigger negative emotions and suffering.

To illustrate this point, let me share an example from my client, Tania.

Tania described herself as a tall, broad, and large woman with a big presence. Prior to our work together, she had embraced an online body-positive movement, learning to love all aspects of her body and gaining a sizable social media following by sharing her views. However, as a budding actor, she faced rejection during a movie audition solely based on her size. This experience left her outraged and saddened for weeks.

In our session, I helped Tania realise that tying her self-worth to her body would continue to cause suffering. Whether she felt good about her body or not, any external disagreement would trigger anger and sadness. This was evident from the trolling comments she received on social media, to which she reacted with anger and an inability to accept.

Through our work together, Tania came to understand that she is not defined by her body, and that it made little sense basing her worth on her physical appearance. Gradually, she realised that loving her body does not need to be another defining aspect of her identity, and she saw that letting go of this attachment was equally important. This newfound perspective brought her closer to a more liberated and accepting view of herself.

Body acceptance is all about seeing your body as it is, without getting too hung up on the details. You don't have to romanticise every imperfection or adore every part of yourself. For instance, you don't have to view your stretch marks as "brave, beautiful warrior stripes," or believe that the shape of your thighs "defines your womanhood." It's perfectly okay to have your preferences and still accept that your body is as it is.

Think of it like owning a car–you might not love it, but as long as it gets you where you need to go, you take care of it. Similarly, you can appreciate the remarkable functions of your body while still acknowledging that you may not love every aspect of its appearance. The key is to recognise that your body doesn't define your worth as a person. When you look in the mirror, you can see it is merely a physical form; a shape. You can also acknowledge your body's functions in a magical way. Think about it: Thousands of systems running each moment and somehow, for the most part, they manage to work and function in harmony. And yet, it's fine to recognise this and still not love certain aspects of how your body looks. Both truths can coexist.

By adopting this attitude, you can treat your body with kindness and care, even if you don't have overwhelming affection for every inch of it. You simply **accept your body as it is without the pressure of having to love every single part**. Embracing this perspective allows you to be gentle with yourself and cultivate a healthier, more realistic relationship with your body.

Many of us already practise acceptance in various aspects of our lives. For instance, consider height or eye colour. Some people might wish to be taller or have a different eye colour, but ultimately, they accept these traits for what they are. They aren't overly obsessed or try to change them, and they certainly don't punish their eyes for not being their preferred colour. So, why should we treat our bodies any differently?

CHAPTER 32:

The worst case scenario

During our sessions, I often ask clients about their biggest fear if they were to let go of their self-loathing and disordered eating habits. Many express concerns that they would continue to gain weight indefinitely. However, as we've previously discussed, weight gain is often linked to the cycle of yo-yo dieting and restrictive eating behaviours. In reality, adopting an intuitive approach to eating can lead to more sustainable weight loss or stabilisation.

However, another common concern is the worry of being judged by others based on your appearance. This fear of external judgement can be a significant obstacle in your journey towards acceptance. Working on this aspect is crucial for healing your relationship with your body and making progress. Addressing these fears may involve discomfort, but in doing so, you may gradually develop greater confidence and self-assurance in your own skin, as was the experience of my client, Aduka.

> *Aduka, a 27-year-old woman shared with me her frustration and intense dislike for her "big fat ass" and the various attempts she had made to reduce its size. When I asked her what she thought would happen if she stopped trying to change it, she expressed her fear that her rear end would continue to grow, and everyone would stare and judge her for it.*
>
> *With her permission, we decided to approach this fear through exposure therapy. Aduka agreed to wear a pair of slightly oversized jeans and add extra padding to make her butt appear as big as she feared. She was then going to bravely embark on a day-long adventure in New York City, riding the subway, visiting cafes, and even meeting a friend without revealing her experiment.*
>
> *In our next session, Aduka recounted her experience. She said, "I spent the entire day with people walking and standing behind me, potentially staring at my big butt. I went to various places, met my friend, and, honestly, it made absolutely no difference to anything. No one treated me differently, and, after a while, I completely forgot about it. Even when I met my friend, I didn't think about it. Later, for a brief moment, I wondered what he might have thought, but then I realised, I just didn't care. I had a really great day."*

This exposure task had a profound impact on Aduka. It allowed her to challenge her fears and anxieties, helping her recognise that the negative judgments she feared were not as significant as she had imagined. Throughout her day in New York City, she came to realise that even if some people held critical thoughts, it didn't affect her sense of ease and self-assurance. It was a significant step forward in her journey towards body acceptance and compassion.

She also had another insightful realisation that she shared with me. She realised in the following days, that she only ever caught glimpses of herself for a few minutes each day, such as whenever she happened to see her reflection in the mirror. The rest of the time, she was so busy doing whatever she was doing that she wasn't even aware of how she looked. She said that this made her question why she would let her self-worth be dictated by those fleeting reflections, when they were such a small fraction of her day.

BITE SIZED THOUGHT

The idea or concern we have about something is often much worse than the reality itself. It's a notion I frequently share with people, in the kindest way possible. I often say that I hope they experience their worst fears, not because I wish them harm, but because I know that confronting their fears head-on can be incredibly transformative. This process allows individuals to realise their inner strength and resilience, leading to a profound shift in their perspective. By facing these fears, they often find that the actual experience is far less daunting than the scenarios their minds had conjured, empowering them to tackle future challenges with increased confidence and a more balanced outlook on life.

Let me share a personal example that taught me the power of facing our worst fears. As a teenager, I always believed that I wouldn't be able to handle anything bad happening to my parents. Just the thought of it would leave me with an overwhelming feeling of fear and an ache in my stomach. It was a fear that had lingered in the back of my mind, until one night when I was just 19 years old, and it became a reality. That night, I received news that my father had been diagnosed with terminal cancer, and he had been given only a short time to get his affairs in order. As I stumbled into my bedroom, my eyes swollen from crying, I couldn't help but feel lost and numb. I gazed at my reflection in the mirror, and I couldn't recognise the person staring back at me. Despite the weight of my worst fears being realised, I was surprised to find that I was coping. It wasn't easy, and there were times when it certainly felt like the world was crashing down around me, but even through the shock and tears, I managed to find a strange sense of calmness within me. It was as if by having to experience my worst fear, it lost its power over me. I felt that a newfound strength had awakened in me, and I knew that I would get through this.

While this story may not directly relate to food and eating, the principle is the same. When we realise the inner resilience we have when faced with adversity, it becomes applicable in all domains of our lives. Perhaps you have experienced a moment when you surprised yourself with your ability to overcome a fear or challenge. If so, maybe take a moment to consider how it changed your perspective on your own inner strength?

LET'S GET WORKING:
Confronting Your Body Fear

INSTRUCTIONS: For this exercise, you'll need your journal and a dash of bravery.

⏳ *As long as it takes!*

In this exercise, we'll confront your deepest fear related to your body, weight, or size.

Following Aduka's inspiring example, create an exposure task for yourself. This task should allow you to face your fear head-on. It could be going out in public wearing something that challenges your body image or engaging in an activity that you've been avoiding due to body-related concerns.

If it seems too difficult or you practically can't do it, then break it down to something more manageable. For example:

If the main challenge is looking in the mirror without criticism, start by setting a timer for a brief period and practice looking at yourself without judgement for that duration.

Or if the main challenge is going out without excessive makeup or grooming, try a "no-makeup" or "low-grooming" day at home before venturing outside without feeling the need for extensive preparations.

Now, reflect on the outcome:
- Were you able to handle it?
- Are you still alive?
- Can you still breathe, move, and think?
- If doing this made you cry or sob, did the crying eventually stop?

Recognize that you can handle the worst case scenario. *Now it's time to move on.*

"It's not about the size you wear, but the way you wear your size."

- Unknown

CHAPTER 33:

Exercise and body image

Exercise is a wonderful source of joy and vitality. Unfortunately, this too has been exploited by the diet industry. What was once a beneficial activity for our physical and mental wellbeing has now become entangled in harmful expectations and judgments. People often fall victim to the belief that exercise, under the guise of health, is entirely benign. Yet, behind this facade lies a dark reality: Engaging in body-punishing physical workouts, rigid macronutrients intake, and holding unrealistic body standards, actually plague our approach to exercise, leaving us feeling degraded and unworthy. Whilst recent years may have seen the trend shift from dangerously low BMI levels to a "strong-not-skinny" narrative, harmful practices still persist.

I am not going to delve too much into how obsessive and compulsive exercising perpetuates the disordered relationship to our eating and body image because I think it is rather evident. Instead, an alternative way of thinking about exercise and how we can approach it will be offered. Spoiler alert: This can be easily narrowed down to a very simple one-line statement: **Focus on movement, not exercise.**

When we exercise solely to change our weight, shape, or size, it becomes no different from following a restrictive diet. We subject ourselves to rigid rules, gruelling routines, and we let our emotions dictate our actions.

When you shift your focus from exercise to **movement**, a newfound sense of freedom awaits you. By letting go of past exercise rules and expectations, you can instead commit to doing whatever feels good for your body in the present moment. There are no limits, no *shoulds* or *shouldn'ts*; just pure acceptance and exploration.

On days filled with boundless energy, you might opt for an intense spinning class. After a hearty meal, a leisurely walk might be more appealing. Weekends could inspire nature walks that unexpectedly transform into delightful four-hour hikes. On tired days, perhaps a simple 20-minute stretching session at home does the trick. Every movement is honoured, and there's no judgement about what's "best" or "worst"–only what brings joy to your body.

Just like with food, when you lift restrictions and expectations about physical exercise, the internal knowingness or wisdom we spoke about is ignited. Once again, when we truly listen to our body, it naturally guides us to the right amount of nourishing movement, telling you what, when, and how to exercise. However, as with food, distinguishing between the body's voice and the conditioned mind's chatter can be challenging at first. The key is to sustain joyful experimentation, let go of guilt and shame, and learn to listen attentively to what truly makes your body feel alive and well.

Harriet is an excellent example of this.

After some gentle encouragement, Harriet made the courageous decision to shift from rigid exercise to simply moving her body in a way that brought joy. For years, she had adhered to a strict and gruelling workout schedule, often pushing herself to the point of burnout. The cycle of intense exercise followed by guilt-induced inactivity had taken a toll on her physical and emotional wellbeing. It was clear that her previous approach to workouts was not serving her.

With a newfound sense of strength, Harriet let go of the old patterns and embraced a more intuitive approach to movement. Daily walks became a delightful habit, and she attended various workout classes when her body felt called to do so. There was no more self-criticism or punishment; instead, she treated herself with acceptance and compassion.

The months passed and when Harriet met me in a follow-up session, her face lit up with joy. "I've been enjoying moving and listening to my body so much that it doesn't even feel like I've done any exercise. However, I just got my blood test back from my annual physical. I have never been heal-

*thier and I've even lost six lbs! I'm not sure how this works,
all I know is that I feel great!"*

Harriet's experience is a testament to the power of letting go
of rigidity and embracing a more loving and intuitive way of
moving. By aligning with her body's needs and finding joy in
movement, she achieved not only a healthier state but also a
greater sense of overall wellbeing.

I hope you're starting to grasp that the secret to transforming
our relationship with our bodies lies in genuine acceptance:
Acceptance of our bodies as they are, not as we wish them to
be. The moment we release the constant need to change our
appearance, a profound shift occurs in our thinking and way
of life. It's a powerful realisation that our body and size have
no bearing on our happiness and contentment; they never did.

When we surrender to this mindset, something remarkable
unfolds. The energy previously spent on self-criticism and
the pursuit of change becomes available for living the life we
truly desire. Moreover, by breaking free from the struggle to
alter ourselves, we also heal our subconscious, convincing it
that we are whole and worthy just as we are. Ironically, many
who reach this point of body acceptance may find that they
naturally start to lose weight, but, unsurprisingly, by this point,
they no longer really care. The illusion that a particular weight,
shape, or size can bring about lasting fulfilment has vanished
and any weight loss is in no way driven by external pressures
but rather fueled by their inner peace.

PART 4

GOING
BEYOND FOOD

"The way you eat is inseparable from your core beliefs about being alive. Your relationship with food is an exact mirror of your feelings about love, fear, anger, meaning, transformation, and, yes, even God."

- Geneen Roth

CHAPTER 34:

Unveiling the layers

Love it or hate it, food is an undeniable and intrinsic part of our lives. Its significance becomes even more apparent when we find ourselves entangled in a difficult relationship with it. Struggling with food and body-related issues can consume our thoughts and energy throughout the day, leaving little room to appreciate other important aspects of life and hindering our sense of purpose, fulfilment, and overall wellbeing.

This was especially evident by my client, Ruth, who came to see me for a few sessions.

Ruth, a rigid and controlled lady in her 70s, sought therapy with me. Externally, her life seemed picture-perfect: Active involvement in her spiritual community, a loving marriage, wonderful children, and a respected job. Everything painted the image of a fulfilled indivi-

dual. However, beneath this facade, a pervasive darkness shadowed her life due to her long-standing struggles with food and her body.

Despite the abundance of blessings in her life, Ruth's demeanour was marred by despair and hopelessness, linked to issues with her body image and consequential food restriction. Her entire life had been tormented by these challenges, preventing her from actually enjoying all the wonders she had been blessed with. While she was aware of this truth intellectually, she wasn't prepared to confront these food-related issues head-on and give up her controlled eating behaviours. Unfortunately, after just three sessions, Ruth disengaged from therapy.

Ruth's case serves as a poignant example that even when we have many fulfilling and positive aspects in our lives, unresolved issues that manifest with body dissatisfaction and consequential disordered eating, can cast a shadow over everything else and be a barrier to growth and wellbeing. Her case once again reflects the complexity of our relationship with food, body image, and self-worth, illustrating that transformation requires readiness and willingness to confront deep-seated beliefs.

However, it's also important to note that **food relationships often go far beyond eating or body image difficulties**. Our eating habits can be influenced by our feelings; they could signify a need for control or demonstrate a lack thereof; they could reflect a relentless pursuit of perfection, shape our self-image, or mirror the battles we wage within ourselves–and these examples only scratch the surface. In fact, even in the absence of challenges related to diets, calorie counting, or body dissatisfaction, food-related issues can emerge. And whilst the outcome may have manifested as disordered eating, it could just as easily have manifested as substance abuse, self-harming behaviours, or a host of other psychological or destructive presentations. A clear example of this is the case of Joshua, whose restrictive eating had nothing to do with his body dissatisfaction.

Joshua, a bright and ambitious 15-year-old, was facing overwhelming pressure at school. With numerous extracurricular activities and mounting academic expectations, he began to exert strict control over his food intake. Choosing mostly simple and plain food, his parents had become worried as he was extremely thin and eating the same restrictive plain meals most days.

In our initial conversations, Joshua struggled to explain why he was being so rigid about what he ate. Initially, we explored whether someone had said something hurtful about his appearance or if he felt pressured to meet a certain image. However, as we delved deeper, it became clear that this wasn't really about changing his physical appearance or having a distorted view of his body at all. Instead, it seemed more like a way for him to cope with the high levels of stress he was experiencing.

For Joshua, food became a tool to bring a sense of order into his life when things felt overwhelmingly chaotic due to stress and pressure. It offered him a small respite from the intense emotions he was grappling with. It was the one

*thing he felt he could control. As we continued our conver-
sations, Joshua shared other aspects of his behaviour that
illustrated his need for control when dealing with stress.
He mentioned that during piano practice, he would closely
monitor the digital clock. If he didn't finish playing his
piece on an even-numbered, he felt compelled to start over.
He explained that he did this for good luck, though he
reassured me that had he wanted to stop this behaviour at
any time, he could have done so. Nonetheless, sticking to
his "even number" method, offered him a sense of control
during his practice. We discussed that this way of thinking
is known as "magical thinking" and is a type of cognitive
distortion that could be fueled by his efforts to cope with
the overwhelming stress to do things perfectly. Our sessions
continued in this direction, focusing on equipping Joshua
with coping skills. Through our work together, he learned
to ease his relationship with food and embrace alternative tools for managing stress, and let go of perfectionist
tendencies.*

Joshua's challenges with food demonstrate how disordered
eating can exist independently from concerns about weight or
physical appearance. In his case, the intense stress and pressure
he faced in his life led him to use food as a tool to regain a sense
of control amidst chaos.

As we have seen, there are cases where the food relationship is
dependent on how someone feels about their body, and there
are examples where the eating difficulties arise without any
clear connection to body weight, shape, or size. However, in

most cases, the relationship to food is more complicated as it is a combination of both of these factors. This was certainly the case for Lottie.

Lottie was a 36-year-old woman, who initially grappled with physical discomfort stemming from her excess weight, driven by a disconnection from her body's needs. Her journey began with overeating, lack of regular exercise, and body image dissatisfaction. Our work together began with learning how to connect with her body, trust in its signals, and adopt healthier eating habits aligned with her body's true needs.

As Lottie progressed, she encountered unexpected emotional hurdles, such as deep-seated negative beliefs about herself (self-hatred, unworthiness, guilt, shame, etc.). It became clear to Lottie that these emotions had nothing to do with eating or body image because they persisted even as she improved her eating habits and felt more at ease with her body.

For the longest time, Lottie had believed that regaining control over her eating and achieving body confidence would unlock her happiness. However, during our work together she began to realise that her happiness really wasn't dependent on her eating habits or body image. In fact, focusing on these concerns had actually served as a distraction. Lottie was so busy focusing on her appearance or perceived lack of willpower–providing a reason to feel bad about herself–that she was never able to face her underlying low self-perception directly. Now, with her disordered eating removed, she was left sitting with her own low self-perception, without an apparent cause. Without being able to blame her eating, her self-disdain was far more unsettling.

And it didn't stop there. Lottie also began to recognise that this underlying emotional turmoil had permeated various aspects of her life. At work, self-doubt and feelings of unworthiness had held her back from pursuing opportunities. In her relationships, she had struggled to express her needs and assert boundaries. Yet her preoccupation with her body and eating issues once again meant she was not able to see how her low self-worth influenced these other aspects of her life. With newfound clarity, she could now see how her distorted thinking patterns had always been present, and she no longer blamed her body for them.

This revelation spurred Lottie to extend her growth far beyond the realm of her eating habits. Healing her food and body issues became the catalyst for a more profound transformation, one that delved into her underlying beliefs about herself. She recognised that this internal work was the key to unlocking an authentic, fulfilling life, unburdened by the weight of disordered eating and negative self-perception.

Lottie's journey sheds light on the intricate relationship between disordered eating, body dissatisfaction, and deeper emotional struggles. Her path to healing revealed that happiness and transformation extend beyond the surface level fixes. It demonstrated that these seemingly all-encompassing difficulties can actually be distractions to a deeper underlying pain. In Lottie's case, addressing her underlying beliefs about her own worthiness. Her experience underscores the importance of recognising the interconnected nature of these challenges.

"The way you think, the way you behave, the way you eat can influence your life by 30 to 50 years."

- Deepak Chopra

Chapter 35:

The necessity of diverse interventions

As we've observed, disordered eating behaviours can manifest for a variety of reasons. Some individuals primarily and solely demonstrate food related issues due to their struggle with body dissatisfaction and mindless eating. This is often a result of societal pressures and the diet industry. From experience, clients who display a strong commitment to change, rapid responsiveness to interventions, stability in other life areas, and significant progress, typically fall into this category.

On the other hand, disordered eating can occur independently of significant body image concerns. In these cases, it can serve as a coping mechanism or a means to divert attention from underlying psychological or emotional challenges. However, for the majority of individuals dealing with eating-related issues, there's often a combination of both body dissatisfaction and non-body-related factors. These non-body-related factors tend to remain concealed in the background, outside of their conscious awareness. What unfolds is a tendency to hyper-focus on the eating and body image struggles. Individuals in this camp believe that achieving a marginally slimmer physique and curbing binge eating will magically resolve their broader problems. This is an excellent way to distract from other under-lying non-body related factors–that is, until they embark on a journey toward better self-nourishment and body acceptance. At this point they inevitably come to realise that such strug-gles only scratch the surface. As they gain freedom from their food and eating concerns, they unearth a deeper truth: their difficulties are intrinsically tied to their own thoughts about themselves, the world, and others, and they have little to do with the size or shape of their body. This newfound awareness empowers them to address the root causes of their challenges, marking a significant step in their recovery journey.

Professionals supporting individuals with disordered eating should be well-prepared to navigate this diverse spectrum of situations, ensuring each client receives tailored and appro-priate support.

BITE SIZED THOUGHT

Whilst it is crucial for professionals helping those with disordered eating to be adaptable and provide personalised support, I believe that most clients benefit from a two-part approach. The initial focus should centre on addressing the physical dimension, ensuring proper nourishment, and reestablishing a connection with the body's needs. Here we focus on the techniques addressed in parts two and three of this book. Once the body is being nourished correctly (approximately 80% of the time), we can confidently shift to the emotional side of disordered eating. By eliminating hunger or physical deprivation as the primary sources of emotional distress, these emotional facets can be explored with greater clarity.

Unfortunately, not every supportive approach considers both of these aspects. Some clients receive nutritional support without exploring the emotional or deeper components, and some follow therapeutic approaches that solely focus on the underlying emotions aspects of the behaviours without addressing the physical needs. In many cases both are necessary.

"The best way to predict
the future is to create it."

- Peter Drucker

CHAPTER 36:

Using food to transform beyond food

Food issues act as barriers in our lives and, as previously discussed, often mask deeper issues, but they also serve as a powerful **gateway to transformation**. As we navigate and resolve food-related challenges, we gain valuable insights and skills that permeate other aspects of our being. When we learn to nourish ourselves with food, we become more attuned to our internal signals and cues in general. Through developing an intimate awareness of our conditioned thoughts and behaviours about food and eating, we start to recognise these patterns in other areas of our lives. The struggles we experience with food become guiding lights, illuminating other areas that need attention and growth.

By fostering a more loving and healthy relationship with food, we unlock the potential for positive change that goes beyond just what's on our plates. When we practise self-care, kindness, and nourishment several times a day through eating, this conditions us to make these acts integral to our being. As a result, we become less accepting of behaviours, whether of ourselves or others, that contradict with this caring approach. In essence, the transformation that begins with food, radiates and becomes a catalyst for positive change in every aspect of our existence. This empowers us to embrace life's possibilities with a newfound sense of joy and purpose. This was especially evident by my client, Rachel, who came to see me for a few sessions.

As Rachel's relationship with food evolved, a profound shift occurred and the self-compassion and love she learned began to spill over into other aspects of her life. In her relationships, Rachel discovered that the same gentleness she showed herself was essential in her interactions with others. She recognised that her struggles with food had, in some ways, affected her ability to fully connect with loved ones. Now, with a newfound sense of empathy, understanding, and honesty, she could be more present and supportive in her relationships.

Similarly, her perfectionism, which had been deeply intertwined with her food issues, revealed itself as a barrier to her personal growth and fulfilment. As she learned to let go of the need for constant control, she found a sense of liberation. No longer confined by the burden of unreali-

stic expectations, she could start to embrace the beauty of imperfection.

These shifts allowed Rachel to approach her work life with a fresh perspective. Her previous drive for being the best had often left her feeling stressed and overwhelmed. Now, she understood that it was okay to make mistakes and that growth often comes through challenges; a truth she had learned by loosening up with food and letting go of the control. This change in mindset not only alleviated her work-related stress but also allowed her to approach tasks with creativity and enthusiasm.

Outside of her professional life, Rachel's new outlook opened doors to pursuing passions she had set aside due to fears of not being good enough. She started painting again, something she had loved in her youth but abandoned when she couldn't meet her own unrealistic standards. Rachel found joy in the process of creating art, regardless of the final outcome.

As Rachel's self-compassion expanded, she also experienced a sense of joy with the world around her. She began to appreciate the beauty in everyday moments, from the vibrant colours of a sunset to the simple pleasure of savouring a home-cooked meal. Her mindfulness practice, honed through her journey with food, allowed her to fully immerse herself in these experiences. And as she learned to care for herself lovingly, she became more attuned to her emotions and began to address unresolved feelings from the past. This emotional growth not only enriched her life but also strengthened her ability to support others through their own challenges.

In essence, Rachel's transformation from a tumultuous relationship with food to one of compassion and understanding had a ripple effect on every facet of her life. Rachel's journey serves as a powerful example of how healing one aspect of ourselves can lead to a cascade of positive change.

It's now time to delve into the steps and discuss the key elements and practices that lead to such transformative results so you can utilise this powerful gateway for yourself.

CHAPTER 37:

The food relationship as your teacher

Food itself is fundamentally neutral. Consider chocolate, for instance. Despite marketing attempts to label it a "guilty pleasure," it holds no inherent moral value. It is us who place the guilt upon it. Consequently, the meaning we give to food is entirely subjective; we relate to a neutral object (food) in a completely subjective manner, tainted by our preconditioned perceptions, thoughts, feelings, and behaviours. This understanding becomes a powerful tool for self-exploration. By recognising the subjectivity of our food choices, we gain insight into our unique perspectives and emotional connections. We can then unveil deeper insights about our values, emotions, and beliefs. Ultimately, this understanding allows us to see how our relationship with food reflects our inner world.

You could argue that everything we perceive is a projection of the meaning we assign to it–a concept prevalent in various Eastern philosophies. However, delving into this profound idea is much simpler when we begin with something seemingly neutral, like food. Let us further explore this concept through the following example of Mark and Sarah.

> *Mark and Sarah came to couples therapy seeking to salvage their struggling relationship. They had been arguing back and forth, each making valid points from their own perspectives, but getting nowhere. The goal was for them to take responsibility for their actions, but they were stuck in a blame game, and things were getting heated.*
>
> *To change the dynamic, I tried a different approach. I asked Mark and Sarah to take a moment and separately write about their relationship with food and eating. They initially looked at me with confused expressions. But after some encouragement agreed to try. It turned out to be an eye-opening exercise for both of them.*
>
> *Mark realised he had specific preferences and a structured way of eating. He wasn't open to trying new foods and tended to eat at specific times, often getting distracted during meals. On the other hand, Sarah recognised that she had a disconnected relationship with food. She tended to go along with what Mark wanted to eat, not voicing her own preferences. Her upbringing taught her to eat what she was given and to not make a fuss.*
>
> *Based on what they learned about themselves through their food reflections, Mark described himself as inflexible*

and controlling, knowing what he wanted and making it a priority. Sarah, on the other hand, saw herself as having difficulty getting her needs met, feeling uncertain about voicing her preferences.

With this new insight, we revisited the issues they had been arguing about earlier. Seeing how their food behaviours mirrored their personalities, they were able to understand how their individual tendencies contributed to their relationship difficulties. This fresh perspective allowed them to have more productive conversations and gain a deeper understanding of each other.

The case of Mark and Sarah illustrates how challenging it can be to identify our individual responsibilities during interactions with others. It's easier to notice faults in someone else's actions rather than honestly examining our own contributions. Using food and eating as a gateway allows us to understand ourselves better, and exploring the emotions we carry provides a neutral starting point to gain insights into what we bring to the table—no pun intended!

If you find yourself thinking, "But food isn't really neutral, as some foods do affect my body, mind, or emotions in specific ways," then here is your reminder: At its core, food remains neutral, simply being what it is. It is people's reactions to food that can differ due to various factors like predispositions, physiology, and circumstances. The fact that some people may have no issues consuming certain foods but others find them problematic is evidence that it cannot be the food itself that causes the issue.

Once this understanding grows, you may see parallels between your eating behaviours and other aspects of your life. Interestingly, there are instances where this connection works in reverse. Some individuals find that eating becomes the sole domain where they can "let go" and are free, while others use it as a means to maintain control when the rest of their lives are stressful and erratic. Through exploring your own relationship with food, you will obtain unique insights into areas of your life that might require attention or opportunities for personal growth. An example that illustrates this is the experience of my client, John.

John, a friendly, hardworking 60-year-old man, came to me because he was a bit overweight and had trouble controlling his eating habits, especially his late-night snacking. His wife suggested he talk to me about changing his behaviour. Although John was overall quite happy, he knew fixing his eating issues would be a good thing.

When we talked about his food relationship, John reported mostly positive experiences. In fact, he described himself as a "foodie" and said he loved different tastes and flavours. As he described this, his face lit up, and he looked like a little care-free kid when he talked about food. When I asked him about other things that brought him joy, he seemed stumped. He enjoyed his work, but he said it was stressful and took up a lot of his time. He was also involved with and arranged events for his church, which he liked, but he admitted that it sometimes felt like more work. He and his wife would go on a 10-day vacation once a year to be with her family, but that was about it.

It turned out that John wasn't used to thinking about joy and doing things just for fun. He explained that his generation was brought up with the mindset of "just getting on with it" without really looking for personal fulfilment. It seemed that his way of having fun and letting loose was really through food. Nonetheless, when I asked him what he'd do if he had all the time in the world, he reeled off a whole list of things that interested him. He said he wanted to play tennis again, something he loved as a young adult but hadn't done in ages. He sang in the school choir as a boy and thought it would be fun to start again. Plus, he had a big pile of books he was yearning to read. As we explored this together, it became clear that John's eating habits were his way of telling himself to add more joy and variety to his life. He hadn't realised it before, but on reflection he felt this made sense.

Over the next few sessions, John and I set goals for him to introduce more joyous and fulfilling activities into his life. After just a little bit of time, he started to make some significant changes. He rearranged his church duties so he could play tennis and he started a men's singing choir at his church. Instead of raiding the kitchen for snacks at night, he spent that time reading. If he felt the urge to overeat, he took it as a sign that he needed to focus on something more fulfilling.

Six months later, John came for our last review session. He was doing great in his tennis league and had lost 15 lbs. By paying attention to the message behind his eating habits and adding more fun and fulfilment to his life, John had transformed both his relationship with food and his overall wellbeing.

Now, it's time for you to pull the pieces together and explore how your eating habits mirror your life and what insights can they offer. The goal is to learn more about yourself, your "hot spots," and look for areas of transformation.

LET'S GET WORKING:
Connecting Your Food Relationship to Other Dimensions

INSTRUCTIONS: For this exercise, you'll need your journal.

⏳ *20-30 minutes*

This exercise asks you to consider your relationship with food and then explore how this extends into various dimensions of your life.

Choose five words that best summarise how you relate to food.

Word Choices:

1. _____

2. _____

3. _____

4. _____

5. _____

Now take a moment to reflect on whether these words have significance beyond your interactions with food. Consider how they align with other facets of your life.

Do you notice these words consistently appearing in your approach to other relationships, activities, or daily routines? Describe the connections you've uncovered between your food relationship and various dimensions of your life. To help you delve deeper into this introspection, consider some of the following examples:

- **Work:** Are there parallels between your work choices and your approach to food? For instance, do you find yourself staying in a job because you are afraid of what might happen if you took a risk? This may be similar to avoiding certain foods out of fear of what might happen if you allowed yourself to eat them. What about your weight? Perhaps you tend to resist change in both scenarios due to apprehension or fear.
- **Relationships**: Do you observe similarities between your relationship dynamics and your food habits? For instance, does your mindless eating mirror instances in your relationships where you struggle to be fully present or engaged?
- **Leisure Activities**: How do your chosen words align with your approach to hobbies and leisure pursuits? Are there similarities between your attitudes toward food and the way you engage in your leisure activities? For instance, does a tendency towards indulgen-

ce or restriction in your food choices reflect in how you approach your leisure time?

- **Self-Care Routine**: Analyse whether the words you selected resonate with your self-care practices. Do they reflect how you nurture your body and prioritise your overall wellbeing? For instance, if you mentioned words like "neglect" or "care," consider how these words might also apply to your self-care routines.

Feel free to draw from personal examples like:

- **Being easy-going**: Which might translate into a less strict approach to your dietary choices.
- **Being frugal with money**: Potentially leading to occasional consumption of cheaper, less nutritious foods.

By examining these connections, you can gain valuable insights into how your food relationship intertwines with various aspects of your life, providing you with a more holistic understanding of your overall wellbeing.

Once you discover that your relationship with food and eating can provide insights into yourself and areas that need attention, the next step is to see that by changing how you approach food, other aspects of your life can also transform, even before you directly address them.

CHAPTER 38:

Eating as your daily practice

Eating serves as a unique and valuable training ground for all aspects of your life because it offers daily opportunities to make conscious decisions about nourishing yourself. It's comparable to learning a new language: You can try your best by attending a weekly class or you can immerse yourself in a place where the language is spoken, providing constant chances for improvement. Positive changes in our food and eating behaviours lead to meeting our basic needs and tuning into our own wisdom regularly, enabling us to get our needs met, foster consistent nourishment, and care for ourselves and, consequently, others.

Furthermore, in contrast to other areas, like relationships, which can be influenced by others' reactions and patterns, eating provides a consistent and one-sided practice. By simply working with our eating habits, we lay the foundation for transformation in other areas of our lives, even before actively addressing them. As we prioritise self-care and attentiveness in our eating choices, these positive changes naturally extend to various aspects of our daily experiences, creating a ripple effect of growth and self-improvement throughout our lives.

In summary, starting with food allows us to infuse our lives with regular opportunities for self-improvement and growth, independent of external influences, making it an ideal foundation for personal development.

This realisation was precisely what Charlotte discovered through her journey.

Charlotte was a 32-year-old woman, who sought help for her eating issues. She was struggling with confusion about how to listen to her body and what to eat, and her self-worth was heavily tied to her weight, shape, and size. Additionally, she felt stressed and unsatisfied with her life situation. Charlotte was stuck in a highly stressful job that she despised and longed to pursue her dream of writing children's books. However, her husband wasn't supportive due to financial concerns.

Once we began working together, Charlotte quickly honed her ability to listen to her body. She learned to distinguish between physical hunger and emotional cravings, and she became adept at stopping when satisfied and choosing foods she truly enjoyed. After just a few months, her approach to food and eating transformed. She no longer weighed herself, realising her value surpassed any number on a scale, and she stopped obsessing about her appearance. This newfound freedom and joy in eating spilled over into every aspect of her life.

As Charlotte stopped seeking validation from others for her eating choices, she also gained the confidence to trust herself in other areas of life. She took a bold step and quit her job despite her husband's discouragement and pursued her passion for writing children's books. To her delight, she secured a publishing deal quickly and her creative writing side business flourished, surprising everyone with its success.

Not only did her career thrive, but Charlotte's relationship with her husband underwent a profound transformation, too. Previously, she allowed him to take the lead, but as she grew more self-assured, she asserted her opinions and argued her case when needed. Their relationship became more equal, and she found the courage to discuss her desire to start a family. Within a year of our work together, Charlotte got pregnant and is now a loving mother to a beautiful little boy.

In just a relatively short span of time, Charlotte's life underwent a remarkable change, all sparked by her decision to change her relationship with food. By prioritising self-care and trusting her instincts, she unleashed a chain reaction of positive developments in her life.

"One cannot think well, love well, sleep well, if one has not dined well."

- Virginia Woolf

CHAPTER 39:

Eating as a reflection of your current state

Your food and eating habits can also be a "canary in the coal mine" that predicts when other areas in your life start deteriorating. I've had clients who started to make significant progress, but then noticed their old patterns resurfaced. They neglected self-care, experienced thoughts and feelings related to low self-worth, or allowed others to dictate their needs and so on. In all these cases, the food relationship worsened. In fact, almost always, **the first area to fall apart was their eating behavior.** You can therefore use your eating habits as a valuable gauge to assess how your life is going. By getting back to basics with food and eating, you can often bring the rest of your life back on track.

Similarly, your eating behaviours can serve as a barometer of your personal growth. Observing how your approach to food and eating has changed becomes an excellent measure of how much you have evolved. This transformation was evident in the case of my client, Ian.

> When Ian sought my help, he had been struggling with food and eating for years, oscillating between restrictive dieting and binge eating episodes, particularly with his main vice, barbecue-flavoured chips. In our sessions, we focused on helping Ian to listen to his body and embrace a mindful approach to eating. Initially, he craved the chips every day and indulged in them regularly. However, as he practised listening to his body's true needs and allowed the chips to be part of the process, something remarkable happened. Over time, Ian developed a newfound sense of freedom and control over his food choices. He realised that he could have the chips whenever he wanted, alongside other delicious and nourishing foods.
>
> Gradually, the chips lost their hold on Ian, and their allure diminished significantly. He reached a point where they no longer had power over him, and they could sit untouched in his house for weeks. Ian's relationship with food transformed, becoming more loving and self-nourishing. During our quarterly check-in, he shared that he no longer craved the chips because he prioritised nourishing his body with nutritious foods instead. He had even thrown away stale chips without feeling deprived.

This example showcases how observing the changes in one's approach to food can become a clear measure of personal growth.

CHAPTER 40:

Movement for wellbeing

Whether referred to as movement or exercise, physical activity possesses the potential to bring about significant positive changes in our lives. However, when driven by fear, self-doubt, or body-related concerns, exercise can transform into a consuming and punishing endeavour. This, in turn, can inadvertently manifest in other areas of our life, leading to behaviours characterised by strictness, severity, or detachment. If you've faced challenges linked to body image and attempted to counter them through compulsive exercise–or if you've observed this struggle in someone else–you may recognise the emergence of obsessive or self-centred behaviours.

This situation closely aligns with the experience of my client, Jackie.

Jackie wrestled with profound body image difficulties, and in her quest to challenge her negative self-perception, she became entangled in compulsive exercise. This fixation drove her to dedicate numerous hours each day to rigorous workouts, and any deviation from this routine triggered feelings of guilt. Unfortunately, this obsession permeated her relationships with friends and family. Jackie's willingness to alter plans to accommodate her exercise schedule alongside her irritability when she was unable to engage in a workout, illustrated the all-encompassing nature of her fixation. This self-centred and unwavering mindset took precedence over the needs and wellbeing of those close to her. Jackie struggled to break free from the grasp of her compulsive exercise habits. Fortunately, with the unwavering support of her family, she came to see me.

When approached thoughtfully, engaging in physical activity provides us with an opportunity to cultivate valuable qualities such as discipline, motivation, and a strong work ethic. It's about understanding the balance between exertion and rejuvenation, knowing when to push ourselves and when to grant our body the rest it needs. Through this process, we're not just participating in a physical routine–we're actively engaging in an act of self-empowerment.

This practice extends beyond the realm of physical health, influencing our choices in other domains. For instance, the commitment to balance and wellbeing in the realm of physical activity can spill over into our professional lives. As we learn the importance of pacing ourselves during a workout, we may recognise how to manage our tasks at work in a manner that avoids burnout. And as we respect the signals our body gives us during exercise, we can become attuned to signs of stress or fatigue in our work environment, prompting us to take breaks and engage in self-care to maintain productivity and mental wellbeing. In this way, the principles of balance and self-empowerment that we develop through physical activity have the potential to enhance our effectiveness and satisfaction in our career pursuits as well.

Furthermore, the lessons we learn from our physical endeavours have a way of rippling into our interactions and decisions. When we decide to forgo a strenuous workout to allow our bodies to recover from aches, we are essentially asserting our ability to prioritise self-care. This very strength then manifests in other circumstances, such as social interactions where we may decline invitations that don't align with our wellbeing, even if they come from well-meaning friends. In this manner, our choices become a reflection of our self-awareness and a demonstration of our ability to set boundaries that safeguard our overall well being. In essence, the act of making conscientious choices in one area of our life, serves as a stepping stone, fostering a mindset of mindful decision-making.

ONGOING TASK

LET'S GET WORKING:
Cultivating Wholesome Choices in Your Life

INSTRUCTIONS: For this exercise, you'll need your journal.

This exercise invites you to embark on a 30-Day Wholesomeness Challenge. For part 1 you will focus specifically on your exercise habits. Part 2 suggests that you extend your experience to other aspects of your life.

Part 1
Begin by reflecting on your current approach to exercise or physical activity. Jot down the characteristics that you believe epitomise your relationship with movement and exercise. Some examples could be:

• Discipline
• Procrastination
• Inconsistency
• Perfectionism
• Laziness

Next, establish a time frame – let's start with 30 days. Commit to fostering more wholesome decisions in your physical activity. This could mean either elevating your commitment, or learning to embrace a gentler pace, depending on what you found.

After 30 days have passed, revisit your reflections and ponder the following:

• How does it feel when you opt for a more wholesome approach?
• Did you miss out on anything significant?
• Did the world unravel when you scaled back on a few workouts?
• Were you able to prioritise a walk over a TV show?

By embracing the positive impact of choosing wholesomeness in your exercise routine, you'll naturally find the motivation to extend these choices to other facets of your life.

Part 2
Following the 30-day mark and your review, embark on this practice again, this time focusing on other areas in your life that you wish to enrich with wholesome choices. For instance:

• Reducing alcohol consumption
• Strengthening connections with loved ones
• Decreasing phone usage
• Prioritising restful sleep

Commit to another 30-day cycle, dedicating yourself to cultivating wholesomeness in the identified area. Return to your journal to chronicle your experiences.

Feel free to repeat this process, shifting your focus to different spheres you wish to enhance. Over time, your life will undergo a remarkable transformation, and you'll find yourself seamlessly embracing numerous wholesome activities.

This exercise offers a blueprint to empower positive change across various domains of your life. The consistency of your effort will serve as the catalyst for a more fulfilled and balanced existence.

Movement also offers a valuable way to transform our lives by helping us become more mindful of our thoughts and their patterns. When we're active, it's hard to focus on other things. This gives us a chance to learn about how we think and how it affects us. For instance, when we're on a strenuous run or other sport activity, it's tough to also think about being sad or down. This doesn't mean we should use exercise to ignore our problems. Instead, we can use it to learn about how **our thoughts are temporary.** We might feel sad, worried, or angry before we start exercising, but during the activity, these feelings seem to fade away. If you notice this, ask yourself: What happened to my thoughts? Where did they go? This simple question can lead to interesting insights about how our thoughts come and go.

To sum up, movement clearly serves as a valuable compass for transforming various aspects of our lives. It aids us in nurturing discipline while also embracing self-compassion, making wholesome decisions, fostering self-acceptance, and heightening our awareness of our thoughts. Regular movement practice enables us to care for our wellbeing, both physically and mentally, leading us towards a more content and vibrant existence.

It's not about perfect. It's about effort. And when you bring that effort every single day, that's where transformation happens. That's how change occurs."

- Jillian Michaels

Chapter 41:

Fostering compassion through our relationship with food

When we embark on the journey to heal our own relationship with food, we often uncover a profound realisation: countless others are needlessly grappling with similar struggles. As we transform our own perspectives, we gain insight into the unnecessary suffering that many around us endure. This leads us to feel great compassion for others undergoing a similar experience. The case example of Ester vividly illustrates this idea, showing how our personal growth can reverberate beyond ourselves.

Ester, a client who had been diligently working with me, sought to address her complex relationship with food.

Over time, she reshaped her eating habits and developed a more accepting view of her body, that was not governed by societal views or demands. This shift not only enhanced her wellbeing but also provided her with a renewed focus and energy to engage more fully with the aspects of life that truly mattered to her.

During one of our sessions, Ester shared an eye-opening encounter. She had reconnected with her old school friends after a year, and noticed their incessant discussions about workouts and diets. Despite being categorised as "slim" or "fit," her friends revealed a deep-seated discontentment and a preoccupation with their physical appearance. Rather than reacting with judgement, Ester empathised deeply. She recognised her past struggles mirrored in their conversations. Her personal journey of growth inspired her to extend a helping hand. She openly shared the insights she had gained during her transformation, hoping to alleviate her friends from the same burdens she had managed to overcome.

Ester's experience highlights an important truth: Our own journey of healing acts as a catalyst for change in others. In the case of disordered eating and body dissatisfaction, the recurring patterns of diets, guilt, and shame that we transcend are mirrored in the lives of those around us. The difference is that with our own newfound capacity to change, we can finally guide those around us to change, too. This interconnected cycle of transformation illustrates the profound impact of healing on both personal growth and the wellbeing of the collective.

CHAPTER 42:

Final thoughts

As you've journeyed with me through this book, I hope you've begun to realise that the transformation of our relationship with food, eating, and body image transcends mere physical health. It has the power to reshape our lives and the lives of those around us in ways we might never have anticipated.

By cultivating awareness of our thoughts and feelings about food, we embark on a profound exploration of our mind, unlocking doors to personal growth. Simultaneously, we learn the delicate art of listening to our body without allowing it to define our entire identity. In this practice, we nurture self-compassion and silence the relentless self-criticism that often shadows us, making way for a brighter and more fulfilling existence.

But our food relationship is not isolated. It serves as a gateway to the wider landscape of our lives. As you start to trust your inner wisdom in matters of nourishment–free from the constraints of conditioned thoughts, identities, and the allure of immediate gratification–you'll find that this newfound wisdom extends its influence to every corner of your life. The joy of living will greet you with open arms, embracing you with nourishment, goodness, and, above all, an abundance of love. May this book serve as the catalyst you've been seeking to embark on your unique transformative journey. A journey toward a healthier and happier relationship with food, eating, your body, and the entirety of your existence.

Remember that real peace is attainable, one small, bite-sized piece at a time.

PART 5

QUESTIONS AND ANSWERS

"Food brings people together on many different levels. It's nourishment of the soul and body; it's truly love."

- Giada De Laurentiis

CHAPTER 43:

Learning through others' questions

During my many years of teaching on the topic of food, eating, and body image, there are several questions, thoughts, and concerns that regularly come up. The final section of this book will address the most common ones. It is my hope that this will provide support and help you troubleshoot some of the thoughts or challenges that you may have as you continue to transform your relationship with food, eating, and body image.

1. Will I lose weight?

This is the million dollar question everyone wants answered. Unfortunately, the best answer I can give is: maybe yes, and maybe not! It depends on so many different factors:

What is your weight when you start doing this work?

You might be underweight when you begin this journey or maybe you're already at your body's comfortable natural weight. Even if your thoughts have not yet transformed, your body has its own idea – just because you want your body to be a particular weight, that doesn't mean your body agrees. Your body's healthy weight range is like your height or eye colour – it just is what it is.

On the other hand, if you're carrying extra weight, you could experience some rapid weight loss as you start aligning with your body. This is quite often seen when you start listening to your body. Then again, you might not. Sometimes, after years of following certain eating patterns, your body's resistance to change might be pretty strong. Your overall health might improve and you could feel better, but these changes might not always show up on the scale.

How long have you been dealing with restrictions, bingeing, diets, and weight fluctuations?

The longer you've been stuck in these habits, the more challenging it can be to break free. It might take some time before you see significant progress. Physically, your body might have become accustomed to holding onto that extra weight. Mentally, those thought patterns and behaviours might have become deeply ingrained.

What are your expectations?

If you're hoping for a quick fix and rapid weight loss, I have to be honest–it might not happen with this approach. Remember, the main goal here isn't shedding pounds. Although weight loss can occur naturally when you provide your body with the right care, it's not an overnight process. You'll need to release the tight hold that your weight and body have on your mind. Over time, you might start to notice real changes happening. By then, the numbers on the scale shouldn't matter to you as much as you thought they would.

2. I'm struggling to discern whether my cravings are from true bodily signals, or if it's my mind playing tricks on me to indulge emotionally. Any advice on how to differentiate between the two?

There are a few unmistakable signs that can help you distinguish between genuine physical hunger and emotional desires for food.

Physical hunger tends to build up gradually over time, evolving and shifting as you move through different levels of hunger. On the other hand, emotional cravings often have a more immediate and compelling pull. The sensation itself is distinctly different. Some describe it as an itch needing to be scratched, a fleeting impulse, or a sudden switch flipping. This contrast can be a helpful guide to discern whether you're responding to true bodily hunger. However, it's worth noting that if your body has grown accustomed to being ignored, you might only become aware of hunger when it reaches an acute stage. In such cases, it could manifest as a sudden, intense hunger or an urgent need for specific foods. This might give the illusion of a craving when, in reality, it's due to a lack of awareness of other hunger cues.

To help with this, it is crucial to immerse yourself in understanding your own hunger awareness scale. This process involves trial and error, regularly checking in with yourself, and adopting a scientist's mindset of experimenting without judgement. Initially, you might confuse emotional hunger with actual physical hunger, but with time you'll become more attuned to your body's signals and deciphering them.

If you're struggling to identify early signs of hunger, here's a suggestion: Try eating at consistent intervals of every three hours for a few days. This can help reawaken your body's hunger signals, leading to a heightened awareness of hunger sensations that extend beyond your previous norm. However, it's important to note that this is the only instance where I recommend eating outside of your body's cues–primarily to reestablish awareness. Once you've reconnected with your sensations, transition back to listening to your body's natural cues.

Your body's desires will evolve based on the level of hunger you're experiencing. When hunger is at its prime, your body will (most likely) naturally crave complete meals made of real, wholesome foods. Interestingly, many clients report skipping snacks because their body is yearning for substantial meals.

Another helpful guide is this: If you find yourself constantly gravitating towards snacks, you might not be fully aligned with your true hunger cues. Of course, there are times when a craving for chips in the morning for breakfast or a preference for grazing throughout the day is perfectly valid. The key is to be honest with yourself. Over time, you'll become adept at distinguishing whether you're reaching for that slice of chocolate cake merely because it's there, or if it genuinely aligns with what your body craves.

3. I often find myself not craving the food I've prepared or that's stocked in my kitchen, even though I usually enjoy it. How should I handle this situation?

There are several factors to consider when addressing this situation:

Embrace the evolution of your tastes.

As you open yourself up to honouring your true cravings, you might notice that even your favourite foods or the items you'd typically desire aren't hitting the mark. This is a positive sign that your palate and preferences are evolving as you become less restricted. If you have easy access to grocery stores and a willingness to experiment, consider altering your food shopping routine. Opt to visit the store more frequently and buy a smaller selection each time. This approach encourages exploration of new foods, ingredients, flavours, and textures.

BITE SIZED THOUGHT

When I lived in London, I had a local grocery store right around the corner from my place. I'd often swing by on my way back from work, yoga, or a walk with my dog, picking up ingredients just before cooking. While I kept some basics at home, I prioritised getting the exact foods I craved when the urge struck. This method is especially beneficial for those who have a history of rigid dieting and automated meal planning. Although it might initially seem overwhelming, it empowers you to be present and decide what serves you best in the moment.

Work around the challenges.

If you're in a situation where you don't have easy access to stores or restaurants, your approach may need some adjustments. This is common for professionals like teachers, doctors, or nurses who need to bring meals from home. In such cases, it's recommended to bring a diverse range of foods that can be stored at work, including options with a longer shelf life. However, be mindful that this approach shouldn't mimic controlling or dieting behaviours, where safety foods are always on standby. The intention should stem from honouring your body rather than resorting to binge eating or control.

Manage the waste guilt.

For many, the idea of wasting food can be a big challenge and can result in eating food you don't actually want. The reality is that eating unsatisfying meals often leads to binge eating later. In such cases, you've essentially wasted the food you didn't truly desire anyway (meaning, it turns to waste in our body) and ended up consuming additional food that does satisfy you. Honest and realistic decision-making can help you avoid this cycle and make choices that genuinely benefit you, free from guilt.

As always: Embrace flexibility.

Remember, the fifth principle is about not having strict rules. Occasionally, if you find yourself surrounded by food you're not particularly excited about, it can serve as an opportunity to practise detachment from always satisfying your immediate wants. Being comfortable with the items at hand is a positive step toward repairing your relationship with food. When you're starting out, balancing these moments with meals that you truly crave will help you find your balance.

4. What characterises a healthy relationship with food?

I'll always remember a moment when I was conducting a training session for a group of professionals specialising in eating disorders. I posed the question, "What does a healthy relationship with food look like?" One of the participants, a seasoned psychiatrist from an eating disorder centre, raised her hand and responded, "It involves having three balanced meals a day–breakfast, lunch, and dinner–along with two snacks. All of them should contain a good mix of protein, carbs, and fats." My initial reaction was, "Well, I must be missing the mark then!" However, what I was really hoping for was an answer that centred on the process rather than the specific content of meals.

The way we approach what, when, and how we eat shouldn't be governed by strict rules or an urge to exert control. It shouldn't serve as a way to manage emotions unconsciously or out of habit, nor should it revolve around body size or a number on the scale. Instead, a healthy relationship with food is less about the specific foods consumed and more about the overall process of eating. It involves making choices based on bodily needs, personal preferences, and wellbeing. It acknowledges occasions where emotions or situations might influence choices, like having cake on your birthday or opting for take-out during particularly overwhelming times. And, perhaps most importantly, it involves eating experiences that are free from judgement, guilt, shame, and feeling unworthy.

When the predominant factor in your food and eating decisions becomes aligned with these principles, and the experience of eating is one free of destructive emotions, that's when you can say you've developed a healthy relationship with food.

5. Does everyone who is overweight have a disordered relationship with food?

No, not necessarily. Some people may carry extra weight because they eat too much (and possibly also drink too much) whilst being less physically active. This doesn't necessarily point to disordered eating habits, and they might not hold a significantly negative body image. For them, adopting a more moderate approach, like a light diet coupled with lifestyle adjustments, can lead to significant success.

It's worth remembering that although diets typically have a high failure rate, around 95%, there is a small percentage (5%) for whom diets do show results. This seems to be most prominent in cases where body image isn't a central concern. Instead, people in this group recognise that their lifestyle might be somewhat "unhealthy" and seek to make positive changes. Interestingly, I've observed that in these cases people often gravitate towards diets that emphasise health-conscious choices and whole foods, rather than overly restrictive plans.

Nonetheless, this highlights a key reason why comparisons with others should be avoided. What works for one person is deeply intertwined with their unique experiences, thoughts, and perspectives. Your journey is your own, so just focus on your own path. It will lead to meaningful and transformative changes.

6. Why do I find it easier to eat less and crave lighter foods when I'm away, especially in warmer places, but struggle to connect with my body and end up overeating when I return home?

It's intriguing how our eating habits can vary depending on our surroundings and circumstances. I'll share a story about a client, who, prior to meeting me, lived in Nepal and followed a certain eating pattern that worked within the local community. However, upon returning to his home in Australia and attempting to replicate the same approach, he felt uncomfortable. This underscores the importance of context. Our bodies have different requirements based on where we are, our activities, and the broader context of our lives. What feels right in one environment may not necessarily translate well to another. Even if you find yourself in the same location, factors like the season, your age, and life situation can all contribute to evolving nutritional needs.

The key advice is to avoid trying to mirror what worked in one setting when you're in a different one. Trust your body's wisdom; it knows what it needs. As the weather turns colder or stress levels rise, or if your physical activity changes, your body might naturally require a slightly higher weight. Resisting this need won't alter reality. Instead, focus on being attuned to your body's present wants and needs rather than fixating on previous outcomes.

Another aspect to consider is the liberating effect of being in a new place. Often, being away offers an opportunity to shed habitual tendencies and daily routines that we associate with being "at home." Travelling can provide a temporary respite from our typical identities and behaviours. Of course, we can't evade our true selves entirely, rather we experience a brief hiatus from these patterns. This might explain why connecting with your body feels easier when you're away–you've essentially taken a step back from your usual self. If this resonates with you, it could be beneficial to seek personalised one-on-one support from a professional. Exploring the recurring identity patterns that hinder your desired life could significantly impact your transformative journey.

Finally, while it's true that you can't escape your own tendencies, certain places might align more harmoniously with your wellbeing. Some individuals revel in cosy, dark winter nights, while others thrive in bright, sun-soaked days. Personally, I discovered that chilly and overcast climates don't quite suit me. Spending more time in warm and sunny locales allows me to apply my own teachings and practices with greater ease. If you have a palpable sense of ease in a particular environment, while it won't resolve all challenges, it can certainly facilitate your efforts in addressing them.

7. Many people make food and eating lifestyle choices and seem to thrive. Why shouldn't I just follow their approach?

It's quite common to observe people making intentional dietary and lifestyle choices in the pursuit of better health or in alignment with their ethical beliefs. Think of vegans and vegetarians, those who embark on juice cleanses, practitioners of intermittent fasting, or those who abstain from particular food groups. These decisions don't necessarily signify a problematic relationship with food. Often, these choices stem from genuine health concerns or moral beliefs, and such individuals would stand by their food decisions even if it would result in weight gain. In these cases, there's no cause for concern. What people choose to eat is akin to their choice of attire, religious beliefs, how they spend leisure time, or any other form of personal expression.

However, it's vital to acknowledge that in some cases individuals may be using the facade of "healthy eating" to mask an underlying eating disorder, and the individual may not even be consciously aware of it. So, while it might be tempting to adopt a health-focused lifestyle endorsed by others (or a group of people), it's imperative to carefully assess if it genuinely aligns with your own needs.

The best advice is to remain open to experimentation while attentively heeding your body's responses. Conduct your own research and explore evidence that might support contrasting scientific perspectives. For instance, if you encounter someone advocating a low-carbohydrate diet, it's worthwhile to explore the benefits of a high carbohydrate intake to gain a comprehensive understanding.

It's also important to be realistic when hearing success stories of others, as there are many variables that could influence the effectiveness of a particular approach. Consider a man who had battled weight issues throughout his life. His weight gain was largely a result of overlooking portion sizes and nutritional content. Once he decided to shed pounds, he embraced an extremely strict low-carb diet. His regimen proved successful for him. But was it the low carb diet that helped or just smaller portion sizes and a strong desire for transformation? Yes, he did lose weight but it's difficult to know what really made the difference. And just because it worked for him, doesn't mean it would work for you.

During one of my talks, a man in his 70s said, "Everyone kept telling me to stop eating bread. It seemed like everywhere I turned, people were talking about how terrible bread is and how we should avoid it. So, I thought I should cut out bread. After about a month, I felt awful! My energy levels plummeted, I felt unsatisfied, and I just wasn't myself. Eventually, I had enough and happily went back to enjoying my bread!" This highlights the importance of tailoring dietary choices to your unique needs and experiences.

In the realm of dietary decisions, the crux lies in prioritising your individual health and wellbeing and placing trust in your body's cues, rather than blindly following what has worked for others.

8. How does the food relationship evolve?

When we first start a relationship with a person, it might be very romantic and full of energy and life. That's the honeymoon period. Then things usually start to change. Life takes over, circumstances are different, and the relationship will either evolve and transform to accommodate this, or it will be reconsidered. **The same is true for food.**

There are cases where women I've worked with experienced the ability to eat whatever foods they wanted right up until menopause, when changes occur and their bodies respond differently. This prompted them to reevaluate their food choices and change their eating habits. Similarly, for those on a food healing journey, the initial approaches that aided in overcoming disordered behaviours, might require ongoing reassessment and adaptation.

From my perspective, a crucial aspect of the food relationship is recognising its dynamic and evolving nature. By cultivating heightened awareness, we can navigate it in a manner that is supportive and nourishing, rather than being confined to rigid notions of what our food relationship ought to be like.

9. Just when I start feeling like I'm making strides, it seems like things take a turn and I'm back to my old habits. Why does this keep happening?

This is actually quite common during the journey. There will be moments when the changes you experience are remarkable. You might even notice foods that used to trigger you are now just sitting untouched in your cupboard for weeks. It's because you're genuinely enjoying nourishing yourself with foods that your body truly needs.

However, there are times when you might feel like you're not progressing at all, and it can seem like you've reverted back to your old ways: self-criticism, categorising foods as good or bad, overeating, or bingeing–it's important to recognise that these periods are significant as well.

I often caution my clients that when things are going smoothly and progress has been made, there's a likelihood that they will soon face a sudden recurrence of old habits or a challenge. And it's not surprising: After spending a considerable amount of time thinking about and consuming food with the sole aim of altering your body, these habits won't simply disappear. They might lie dormant temporarily but then they resurface unexpectedly, causing disruptions. While it might feel discouraging, this is precisely where the most substantial work and transformation occurs. It's easy to fixate on major breakthroughs, but it's in the small, everyday adjustments that genuine change truly takes root!

It can be useful to think of progression in terms of a spiral rather than a linear process. It's not that you are 'done' with certain things and then move on without ever facing them again. Rather, the same things do come back again and again, and it's just that each time they become more and more refined. As you revisit certain challenges or aspects of yourself, you do so with greater wisdom, insight, and self-awareness each time.

10. I often plan my meals based on my weekly budget, so I'm curious whether this approach could end up costing more?

Once again, this boils down to honesty and intent. If your takeaway of the technique is that "Dr. Romi said that I should eat whatever, whenever," then you have missed the core message and you will likely find yourself not only exceeding your budget, but also overeating beyond what your body truly needs.

In reality, clients often share a surprising revelation when they genuinely tune into their bodies. They've noticed that they require much less food than they previously assumed. In fact, this is often a struggle that many people report! I frequently hear from clients that they find themselves missing out on certain foods because they're not eating as much anymore. It's like their eating habits have shifted. They're naturally focusing on nourishing their bodies with real foods and respecting their hunger cues, so many of those snack cravings have diminished. Admittedly, choosing items like fresh produce may increase your weekly food expenses slightly, but it's possible that you'll spend less on heavily processed keto bars, meal replacement shakes, takeout dinners, and the like.

Finally, clients have noticed that once they stop eating when they are truly full, they find themselves having left-overs regularly. Suddenly, the pizza you used to finish in one go, lasts two meals. You may find that you end up getting more bang for your buck each time you make or order food.

11. I want to work on changing my relationship with food and eating but I really struggle with other people's judgements and comments. What should I do?

It can be hard work to change your relationship with food and eating, especially when you're confronted with the judgements and comments of others. Below are effective strategies you can use to handle these situations with grace and confidence.

Establish a clear boundary phrase.

Prepare a boundary phrase in advance to respond to judgemental comments about your food or body. For example, you might say, "I value your opinion, but my body and food choices are personal matters. Please don't bring this up with me again." And stand your ground with your boundaries. If someone persists or continues to make comments, assert your boundaries firmly. You could reply, "I've already expressed how I feel about your comments on my body or what I eat. If we can't have a respectful conversation, I'm going to walk away."

Listen, smile, and walk away.

If you're not comfortable confronting the person directly, simply listen to their comment, offer a smile, and gracefully walk away. Later, reflect on their behaviour and try to understand their motivations. What is their relationship with food, eating, and body image? Where did it come from? How much do they struggle with the beliefs they have? Can you drop the hurt, anger, or shame you felt when they made their comment, and simply feel compassion for them? You are working to make changes in your life, but it seems they don't even have the capacity or desire to think about making changes.

Use humour or shock as a defence.

Once you've built up your confidence and self-assuredness, you can employ a more sarcastic or even confrontational approach to deflect comments. For instance, responding with exaggerated self-criticism like, "Yeah I'm just so disgusting–I have no self control and I am just so gross", can catch people off guard and discourage further comments. A word of caution, though–**only use this if you're truly confident and know you don't believe the statements you're making.**

Remember, your journey to improve your relationship with food is about your personal growth and wellbeing. While the judgements of others can be hurtful, ultimately, their opinions shouldn't define your path. Stay focused on your own progress and take pride in the positive changes you're making in your life.

12. I have a health condition (diabetes, high blood pressure, heart disease) and have been told by my doctor to restrict certain things. Does that mean I can't use this approach?

Having a health condition like diabetes, high blood pressure, or heart disease requires careful consideration, but it doesn't mean you can't apply these strategies. In fact, research indicates that intuitive and mindful eating can lead to improvements in health markers and management for various conditions.

It's crucial to remember that **honouring your body involves developing a deep connection with what serves it best**. While others can offer evidence-based advice, only *you* truly understand your body's responses. Take diabetes as an example: If you've been advised to restrict sugar, explore what that means for you specifically. Is a small amount of sugar manageable, or do different sweeteners affect you differently? How does your body react to sugars from fruits versus sugary snacks? Does the impact of sugar change if eaten after a balanced meal? Approach these inquiries with curiosity, kindness, and love.

Many diabetics adopt an all-or-nothing mindset, similar to traditional dieters. If you believe complete avoidance is the only option, certain foods gain an undue power, often leading to intensified cravings. Instead, consider allowing yourself controlled portions of foods you enjoy. For instance, indulging in a few chocolate cubes after dinner could satisfy cravings more effectively than suppressing them throughout the week and then overindulging later.

Remember, if you're dealing with a pre-existing health condition, your path might include adaptations and detours. However, you remain the steward of your health. By experimenting within the parameters set by your healthcare provider, you can discover what suits you best without deprivation. A health condition doesn't define you or limit your potential; it offers an opportunity to deepen your understanding of your body and become your own expert.

13. With so much contradictory information and a society that promotes thinness, how can I ensure my kids don't succumb to disordered eating?

If you have the awareness to ask this question, you are already on the right track to helping your kids develop a healthy relationship with food, eating, and their body! Yes, there are many external factors outside of the home that could mean that even if you do everything "right," your child may still experience disordered eating patterns. However, if their home life is one that openly communicates about the importance of eating according to what the body needs, does not place food as a reward or punishment, and generally cultivates a positive environment around food (which also includes saying no at times),this will be a huge protective factor as they navigate external influences.

Similarly, a home environment that does not overemphasise body size, shape, or judgments of different body types, can also shield your kids from negative societal influences. Furthermore, promoting gratitude for the body's functionality and its unique role in enabling life experiences can foster body satisfaction. Remember, this it's about promoting a detachment from rigid physical ideals, and accepting and understanding that bodies naturally change over time.

Finally, my biggest recommendation to parents is for them to explore and transform their own relationship with food and eating. Kids pick up on even the most subtle behaviours. You may not even be aware of how damaging some of your own thoughts, feelings, and behaviours concerning eating or your body are until you explore it. Remember, so much "disordered" behaviour is normalised in our culture. It's important to be honest with yourself. By transforming your own food and body relationship, you can finally help others from a place of authenticity.

14. Is this appropriate for patients suffering with clinical eating disorders?

This is one of the questions I get asked the most and the honest answer is that sometimes it is, but often it is not.

If someone is struggling with Anorexia Nervosa and has a very low body mass index (BMI), I would suggest not to use many of the strategies discussed here. Low BMI is associated with a significant impact on brain function. Research shows that malnutrition can cause cognitive deficits, including impaired memory, attention, and problem-solving abilities. These deficits can make it difficult for patients suffering with anorexia to understand and apply many of the principles discussed. More importantly, this approach is all about taking complete responsibility for one's health and wellbeing. Sadly, individuals struggling with anorexia commonly lack the desire to take responsibility for themselves and their recovery. As a result, there is often resistance to seeking help, denial of the severity of their illness, or a reluctance to engage in treatment. Without a willingness to take responsibility for one's own health and wellbeing, you cannot make the necessary changes to develop a healthy relationship with food, eating, and body.

Similarly, there is some evidence to suggest that individuals presenting with Bulimia Nervosa, in which there are significant binge-eating episodes followed by purging (through self-induced vomiting, excessive exercise, or the use of laxatives), can also impact cognitive functioning. Although the exact nature of these deficits is not fully understood, the research suggests these individuals may have difficulties with cognitive tasks that require sustained attention, working memory, cognitive flexibility, and decision-making processes may be impaired. That being said, this is not the case for all individuals with bulimia. I have successfully worked with many motivated clients who are willing to take responsibility and want to change their food and eating habits. If this is how the client presents and they are committed to stop risky behaviours (i.e. committing to avoid any type of self-harm, including excessive purging) then this approach can be extremely transformative when properly applied.

I once had a client who came to see me because she was purging up to five times a day and had fainted on the train. I discussed my approach but explained that I couldn't work with her unless she took the purging completely "off the table." To help her decide if this was something she wanted to do, I discussed the dangers of excessive purging and also shared the research that has shown that vomiting cannot get rid of all the calories ingested, even when done immediately after eating. Once she realised that she was causing herself significant harm, that her method was not completely effective, and she would not be able to work with me, she made her choice. From that day, she never purged again.

A key factor for success is the individual's willingness to take responsibility for their own life. However, in certain cases where a patient is severely struggling with an eating disorder, some treatment techniques may inadvertently undermine this sense of agency. Patients may be told that they are not in control and are unable to make decisions for themselves. In some instances, terms such as the "anorexic brain" are used to describe an external force that influences their behaviour and emotions surrounding food and eating. A common one is for patients to be told to name their eating disorder. You may hear them say things like "ED (a nomenclature for "eating disorder") is showing up again." While such techniques may be necessary to prevent a patient from dying, they can also leave patients feeling victimised and disempowered. This can make it difficult for patients to take ownership of their own recovery later in the process. There are some treatment programs that attempt to balance the need for externalisation with the importance of internal empowerment, but this approach is not yet standard practice.

If you work with individuals in a clinical setting, it's crucial to consider if the treatment approach you offer encourages personal responsibility for recovery and if the individual is physically capable of engaging in the approach. Once weight has been restored and risks are minimised, this approach can be a valuable next step in their recovery journey. At the very least, the ideas presented here serve as a helpful tool for family members and clinicians to examine their own relationships with food, eating, and their bodies.

15. My eating is OK but I have other difficulties in my life. Is it still worth me following these tools?

Absolutely. The tools presented in this book hold immense value even if your eating habits seem satisfactory. The journey to transform our relationship with food extends far beyond the dining table–it serves as a gateway to profound self-discovery and personal growth. While your eating habits might appear fine, the techniques outlined here can provide a unique vantage point for understanding your thought patterns, emotional triggers, and decision-making processes. These insights, acquired through exploring your food relationship, can seamlessly extend to other aspects of your life, shedding light on hidden challenges and facilitating positive change.

Consider this: Our approach to food often mirrors our broader life habits and attitudes. By honing your mindfulness around food and cultivating a compassionate perspective, you'll develop a powerful toolkit to navigate challenges beyond the realm of eating. Just as healthy eating fosters self-care and balance, these tools empower you to apply the same principles to your relationships, work, and overall wellbeing. Ultimately, embarking on this transformative journey allows you to unearth hidden aspects of yourself and equips you with adaptable skills that can uplift various dimensions.

"Food is maybe the only universal thing that really has the power to bring everyone together. No matter what culture, everywhere around the world, people get together to eat."

- Guy Fieri

Acknowledgements

It is with immense joy and gratitude that I present this book–a result of unwavering encouragement that brought its pages to life and infused them with profound meaning. None of it would have been possible without the support and guidance of many individuals.

First and foremost, I would like to express my deepest appreciation to my dear husband, whose positive and mindful relationship with food and body was my inspiration in those early days. I thank you for serving as my initial subject of investigation, even if you weren't aware of it! Mostly, I thank you for being a constant guiding light in my life.

I would also like to thank my children, who provided me with a personal platform to practise the principles I teach to other parents. Your openness and adventurousness with food have been a source of great joy. May your food relationship continue to flourish and be your constant reminder to infuse your life with compassion, equanimity, and love.

To all of my clients who have trusted me with their stories and experiences, I offer my sincere thanks. Your unique journeys have allowed me to gain valuable insights, and to continually refine and enhance my approach. There was a time where I believed I was the one helping you, but experience has shown me that, in fact, it was always the other way around. Thank you for trusting in me and contributing to my growth.

To the many teachers who have influenced my life and work, I extend my deepest appreciation. Your wisdom and guidance not only enabled me to develop my professional skills but, more importantly, showed me how to see the world in new and profound ways. I am forever indebted to you all.

A special tribute is reserved for my editor and dear friend, Hannah. Your ongoing support, dedicated encouragement, and countless hours of collaboration have played a pivotal role in refining the essence of this book. Your presence in my life is truly a gift.

And finally, to the numerous others who have contributed to this endeavour–there are simply too many to name–my gratitude is boundless.

As these pages reach readers, my earnest hope is that the insights they contain resonate deeply and spark transformative change, inner harmony, and enduring peace for everyone.

Suggested Reading

This list features 20 books on intuitive eating, mindful consumption, and related topics. These texts, along with many others beyond this list, have profoundly shaped my exploration of our relationship with food, our bodies, and life in general. Their wisdom continues to enrich my journey and serves as a valuable resource for those seeking a healthier, more mindful connection with food, body, and life. I invite you to explore these transformative works, each holding a wealth of wisdom for your path to wellbeing and self-acceptance.

- "Intuitive Eating" by Evelyn Tribole and Elyse Resch (1995)

- "The Rules of Normal Eating" by Karen Koenig (2005)

- "Normal Eating for Normal Weight" by Sheryl Canter (2005)

- "Mindful Eating" by Jan Chozen Bays (2009)

- "Diets Don't Work" by Bob Schwartz (2009)

294 Bite Sized Peace

- "Eat What You Want, Eat What You Eat" by Michelle May (2009)

- "Beyond Chocolate" by Sophie Boss and Audrey Boss (2006)

- "Health at Every Size" by Linda Bacon (2010)

- "The Yoga of Eating" by Charles Eisenstein (2010)

- "Body Respect" by Linda Bacon and Lucy Aphramor (2014)

- "The Intuitive Eating Workbook" by Evelyn Tribole and Elyse Resch (2017)

- "The Intuitive Eating Workbook for Teens" by Elyse Resch and Evelyn Tribole (2020)

- "How to Eat" by Thich Nhat Hanh (2014)

- "Eat What You Love, Love What You Eat with Diabetes" by Michelle May (2012)

- "Beyond Temptation" by Sophie Boss and Audrey Boss (2012)

- "On Eating" by Susie Orbach (2021)

- "Anti-Diet: Reclaim Your Time, Money, Well-Being, and Happiness Through Intuitive Eating" by Christy Harrison (2020)

- "Intuitive Fasting: The Flexible Four-Week Intermittent Fasting Plan to Recharge Your Metabolism and Renew Your Health" by Dr. Will Cole (2021)

- "The Intuitive Way to Wellness: A 28-Day Plan to Heal Your Body, Mind, and Soul" by Shannon Beador (2021)

- "The No-Brainer Nutrition Guide For Every Runner: How to Fuel and Train Right" by Jason Fitzgerald (2022)

"Motivation is what gets
you started. Habit is
what keeps you going."

- Jim Ryun

Printed in Great Britain
by Amazon

42117224R00172